Kayakers explore the western shores of Vancouver Island.

CANADA'S
Incredible Coasts

Prepared by the Book Division
National Geographic Society, Washington, D.C.

CANADA'S INCREDIBLE COASTS

Contributing Authors: Tom Melham,
    Thomas O'Neill, Cynthia Russ Ramsay,
    Gene S. Stuart, Jennifer C. Urquhart

Contributing Photographers: James P. Blair,
    John Eastcott and Yva Momatiuk,
    Michael Melford, James A. Sugar

Published by The National Geographic Society
Gilbert M. Grosvenor,
    President and Chairman of the Board
Michela A. English,
    Senior Vice President
Robert L. Breeden,
    *Executive Adviser to the President
    for Publications and Educational Media*

Prepared by The Book Division
William R. Gray, *Director*
Margery G. Dunn, *Senior Editor*

Staff for this Special Publication
Gene S. Stuart, *Managing Editor*
Charles E. Herron, *Illustrations Editor*
Suez B. Kehl, *Art Director*
Carolinda E. Hill, *Senior Researcher*
Timothy H. Ewing, William T. Spicer,
    Researchers
Richard M. Crum, Carolinda E. Hill,
    Tom Melham, Cynthia Russ Ramsay,
    Jennifer C. Urquhart, *Picture Legend Writers*
Kevin P. Allen, Gary M. Johnson,
    Joseph F. Ochlak, Daniel J. Ortiz,
    Martin S. Walz, *Map Research and Production*
Isaac Ortiz, *Map Relief*
Sandra F. Lotterman, *Editorial Assistant*
Artemis S. Lampathakis, *Illustrations Assistant*

Engraving, Printing, and Product Manufacture
George V. White, *Director*,
John T. Dunn, *Associate Director*, and
Vincent P. Ryan, *Manager*,
    Manufacturing and Quality Management
Lewis R. Bassford,
    Production Project Manager
Heather Guwang, Richard S. Wain, *Production*
R. Gary Colbert, Karen F. Edwards,
    Elizabeth G. Jevons, Teresita Cóquia Sison,
    Marilyn J. Williams, *Staff Assistants*

Lucinda L. Smith, *Indexer*

*PRECEDING PAGES: Swallow Tail Light flashes
atop New Brunswick's Grand Manan Island as
mist drifts over the Bay of Fundy and veils the sun.*
BILL BROOKS / MASTERFILE

BARBARA BRUNDEGE / EUGENE FISHER

■ *Day dawns early in Arctic summer. Two hours after midnight, with the sun blazing above the horizon, an Inuit hunter and his dogs cross sea ice near Baffin Island.*

5

Ellesmere Island

ARCTIC OCEAN

Beaufort Sea

ALASKA
(U. S.)

Banks Island

Cornwallis Island

U. S.
CANADA

Victoria Island

YUKON TERRITORY

★ Whitehorse

ARCTIC CIRCLE

NORTHWEST TERRITORIES

★ Yellowknife

R o c k y   C o a s t   M o u n t a i n s

BRITISH COLUMBIA

Hudson Bay

Queen Charlotte Sound

ALBERTA

Vancouver Island

Edmonton ★

MANITOBA

Victoria ★

SASKATCHEWAN

PACIFIC OCEAN

Regina ★

ONTARIO

CANADA
U. S.

Winnipeg ★

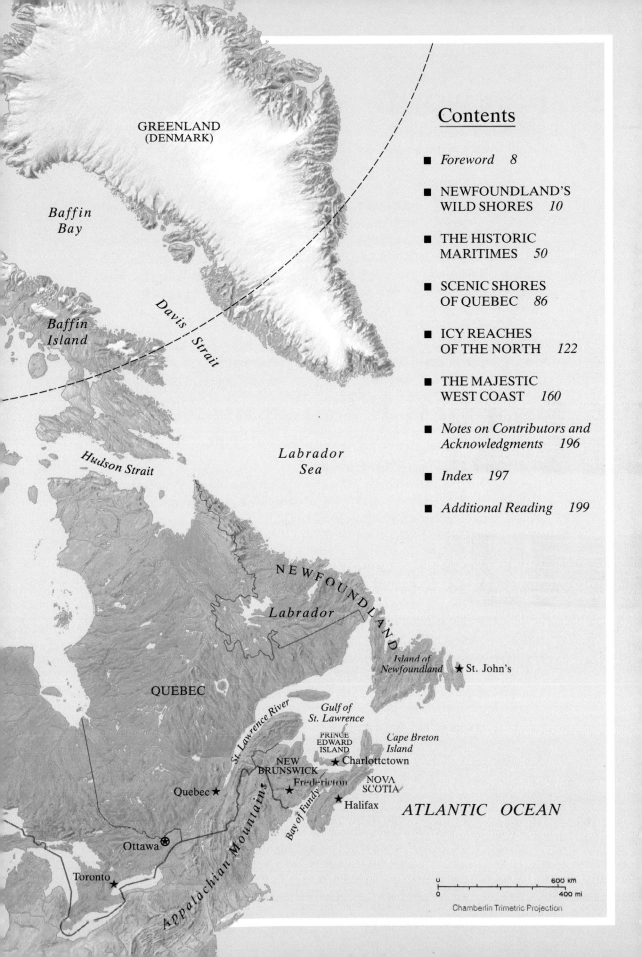

GREENLAND
(DENMARK)

Baffin
Bay

Baffin
Island

Davis Strait

Hudson Strait

Labrador
Sea

NEWFOUNDLAND

Labrador

Island of
Newfoundland ★ St. John's

QUEBEC

St. Lawrence River

Gulf of
St. Lawrence

PRINCE
EDWARD
ISLAND

Cape Breton
Island

Charlottetown ★

NEW
BRUNSWICK

Fredericton

NOVA
SCOTIA

Quebec ★

Halifax ★

Bay of Fundy

ATLANTIC OCEAN

Ottawa ⊕

Appalachian Mountains

Toronto ★

0 ——— 600 km
0 ——— 400 mi

Chamberlin Trimetric Projection

Contents

Foreword

By Gilbert M. Grosvenor
President and Chairman, National Geographic Society

A MONG MY FONDEST MEMORIES—from childhood to the present—are those of summers I spent in Baddeck, Nova Scotia, at the house built by my great-grandfather Alexander Graham Bell, who was president of the National Geographic Society from 1898 to 1903. There, on Bras d'Or Lake, I learned to sail on the yawls *Elsie* and *White Mist*. As we would sail into snug harbors, I recall that I gazed with fascination into water so clear you could see to a depth of 20 feet.

Since those early years, my love of sailing and of Canada has led me to explore much of the country's coastal waters. I have traveled the length of the Inside Passage in British Columbia and voyaged along the St. Lawrence River in Quebec. I have navigated rough seas off the rugged coasts of Newfoundland and sailed around Prince Edward Island's gentler shores. Adventuring with my father, Melville Bell Grosvenor, we challenged the shifting shoals and treacherous currents off Nova Scotia's Sable Island—one of the "graveyards of the Atlantic." Some 25 years later, the thought of exploring Sable, then departing safely aboard *White Mist* still excites me.

More recently, while on a trip to the North Pole, I was overwhelmed as I flew above Canada's Arctic Archipelago, a vast wilderness of more than half a million square miles. Below me stretched islands, ice, and water as far as the eye could see. When I landed at the town of Resolute, on Cornwallis Island, I was surprised to find that this spot—500 miles north of the Arctic Circle—is the destination of several hundred planes a month in summer. Despite the harsh climate, people come here for the dramatic vistas, the rich natural resources, and the possibility of high adventure.

The continuing efforts by Canada to preserve its scenic shores and to protect its natural resources are admirable. As a result, there are many areas that have retained their original character. The Bras d'Or Lake region has changed little since I was a small child. It still possesses the physical beauty that drew my ancestors there in the 19th century. And today, my children are the fifth generation of our family to sail the pristine waters near Baddeck.

This volume is a celebration of Canada's treasured coasts. It honors the generations who have lived along these shores, and welcomes visitors who, along with me, will never tire of exploring their many wonders.

Aboard White Mist, *Gil Grosvenor, his wife, Wiley, and children* ■
Hovey and Graham (in striped shirt) enjoy a day of sailing at
Baddeck, in Nova Scotia. The Elsie, *now used by the town as*
a training vessel for young people, follows close behind.

Newfoundland's Wild

■ *Of the sea, by the sea, for the sea: Spirits buoyed by a good day's catch, a trinity of inshore*

Shores

By Tom Melham
Photographs by John Eastcott and Yva Momatiuk

fishermen heads home to Bay de Verde with the traditional Newfoundlund mainstay—codfish.

".. . it is the land God gave to Cain."

—Jacques Cartier, 1534

"Na, na, me son—that's God's country, that is."

—Newfoundland fisherman, 1990

F OR FIVE CENTURIES AND MORE, voyagers to rock-ribbed Labrador have damned and praised its coast—sometimes simultaneously. Few ignored it. How could they? Craggy and windswept, guarded by icebergs and submerged rocks, this ancient prow of a continent juts boldly into the North Atlantic as if challenging it and its notorious weather to do their worst. They often oblige. Storms commonly rage for weeks on end, encasing Labrador in brutal fogs, chill winds, and brittle ice. Even sunny days unsettle visitors with mirages that flip offshore islands upside down, or wrap the horizon in a wavy, desertic haze. Then there's the Labrador Current—Iceberg Alley—sweeping down from Baffin Island and northern Greenland with its cargo of white megaliths. In April 1912 the *Titanic* succumbed to an alley-borne berg. Ocean currents—both the frigid Labrador and the warm Gulf Stream—help explain why, though Labrador occupies the same latitudes as Great Britain, southern Scandinavia, and other north temperate regions, its climate is singularly stern.

Yet Labrador is hardly sterile. Its namesake current ferries south an endless supply of mineral nutrients and plankton, which power food webs that keep this coast awash in salmon, arctic char, and trout, as well as harp and harbor seals. Some 500 miles off Labrador's southeastern tip, above a tongue of continental shelf known as the Grand Banks, this nutrient-rich current collides headlong with the northward-wending Gulf Stream; the result is one of earth's richest fisheries. Cod and halibut, tuna and swordfish, tiny capelin and giant whales, seals and seabirds, all feed here. In 1497 this abundance so impressed the Venetian John Cabot, exploring for England, that he reported fish could be taken without hooks or nets, merely "in baskets let down with a stone."

Between this offshore bonanza and Labrador's grim profile lies the isle of Newfoundland: a stony wedge that, like a just-popped champagne cork,

■ *Rugged as the North Atlantic itself, bare-boned granite cliffs carved by glaciers endure along Saglek Bay. Distant icebergs ride the Labrador Current.*

seems lately burst from the bottleneck of the Gulf of St. Lawrence. Like Labrador, Newfoundland stands rumpled and furrowed, so bony and glacier-scraped that residents affectionately call it "the Rock."

Together, mainland Labrador and island Newfoundland constitute a political unit: Newfoundland Province, Canada's seventh largest, embracing some 156,000 square miles (two-thirds of them in Labrador) and nearly 600,000 residents (nine-tenths of whom live on the Rock). It is Canada's most easterly bastion: Its capital city of St. John's lies closer to Ireland than to the Canadian heartland of Manitoba, nearer Reykjavik than Chicago. Emotionally, too, Newfoundland faces east; in some ways its history has been more British than North American.

Ironically, England, after a flurry of colonizing efforts in the 17th century, discouraged settlement and withheld government from Newfoundland, treating it as a private wharf for West Country fleets that fished the Grand Banks in summer and returned home each winter. But this migratory fishery left a trickle of settlers behind every winter, and eventually Britain had to concede their existence. The same frictions prevalent at home were imported to this half-formed colony: Protestant versus Catholic, Irish versus English, landed elite versus a labor force of landless and largely illiterate poor. Fishing merchants ruled Newfoundland through a truck, or barter, system, in which they provided food and equipment to fishermen, who paid them in fish. Since the merchants alone set prices, fishermen remained eternally in their debt. Yet despite such inequities and the revolutionary example set by the nearby American colonies, Newfoundland remained remarkably, unshakably British. Even today, while some residents of Irish descent deride the Union Jack as "the Butcher's Apron," many other Newfoundlanders fly it in preference to Canada's Maple Leaf or their provincial flag.

"*I*T DOES SEEM PARADOXICAL," allows historian Leslie Harris, former president of Memorial University in St. John's. "Newfoundland fishermen were independent in that they cut themselves off from the Old World and worked very hard. But they made themselves slaves to a vicious economic system."

Newfoundland author Patrick O'Flaherty offers an explanation: "Society here was much more quiescent, more peaceful, more accepting than in the States. Much more rudimentary; there was an unwillingness of the people to assert their rights until well into the 19th century. The humble and poor are conservative by nature."

Newfoundland's rich seas, harsh climate, and rocky soil made fishing the only option for such people. They scattered themselves along the shore to better share in their common resource. Thus the island gave rise to innumerable outports, disparate fishing communities often connected only by the sea they

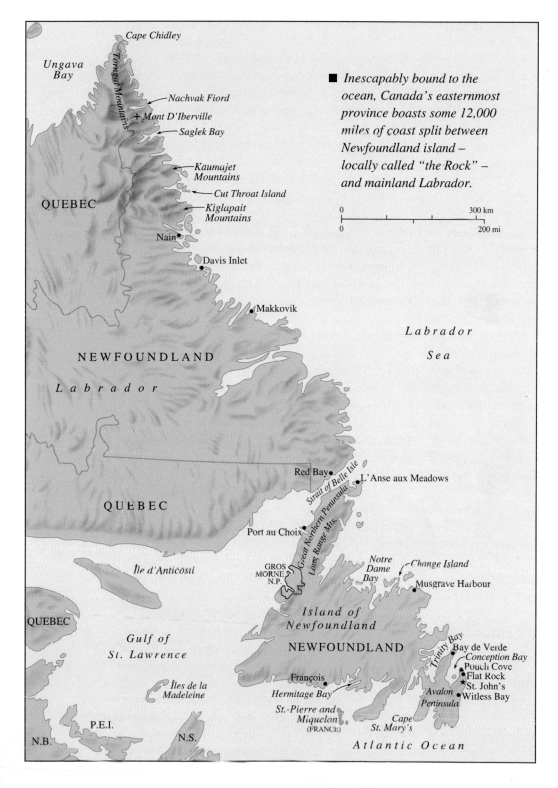

Cape Chidley

*Ungava
Bay*

Torngat Mountains

Nachvak Fiord

+ Mont D'Iberville

Saglek Bay

Kaumajet
Mountains

Cut Throat Island

Kiglapait
Mountains

Nain•

•Davis Inlet

•Makkovik

QUEBEC

NEWFOUNDLAND

Labrador

QUEBEC

Île d'Anticosti

Red Bay•

L'Anse aux Meadows

Strait of Belle Isle

Great Northern Peninsula

Port au Choix•

Long Range Mts.

GROS
MORNE
N.P.

*Notre
Dame
Bay*

Change Island

Musgrave Harbour

*Labrador

Sea*

■ *Inescapably bound to the
ocean, Canada's easternmost
province boasts some 12,000
miles of coast split between
Newfoundland island –
locally called "the Rock" –
and mainland Labrador.*

| 0 | | | 300 km |
| 0 | | | 200 mi |

*Island of
Newfoundland*

NEWFOUNDLAND

Trinity Bay

•Bay de Verde

Conception Bay

Pouch Cove
•Flat Rock
★St. John's
•Witless Bay

*Avalon
Peninsula*

QUEBEC

*Gulf of
St. Lawrence*

*Îles de la
Madeleine*

François•

Hermitage Bay

St.-Pierre and
Miquelon
(FRANCE)

*Cape
St. Mary's*

P.E.I.

N.B.

N.S.

Atlantic Ocean

fronted. Land communications were primitive until the late 19th century, when a transinsular railway was completed. Today Newfoundland roads remain capricious, leading you along one side of a peninsula but ignoring the other, or marooning you at a gap that logically would be paved. Not until 1965, with completion of the Trans-Canada Highway across the island, did a continuous road efficiently link one side with the other. Even now, Newfoundlanders born on one part of the island can have difficulty understanding islanders from just a hundred miles away. By and large, this province has remained a place of the sea, remote even from itself.

Dr. Harris, who grew up in a Newfoundland outport during the 1920s and '30s, recalls his town as "about 300 people living peaceably, but essentially in social anarchy. Until I left to come to university, I had never seen a policeman. I had never seen a magistrate nor a judge nor any representative of government, with the one exception of postmaster—postmistress, actually. We lived without the ministrations of government or law. And yet in the hundred or so years our community had existed, there had been almost no violence, no significant incident of lawbreaking. You would have expected the opposite, with the absence of authority. But the communities were very peaceable and lawabiding. People worked together. Life was totally different from the six-gun development of the American West. I've often wondered why."

Newfoundland's contradictory combination of independence and passivity helps explain why this, one of the New World's first attractions, never parlayed its head start into a position of colonial leadership. Let other rivermouth islands—such as Manhattan—diversify. Newfoundland would pursue a single-minded economy based on fish, fish, and more fish. It would neither lead nor join the Maritime Provinces, but go its own way as a colony, later as a semi-independent dominion. Only in 1949—nearly 500 years after Europeans began regularly fishing its waters—would it join the Canadian fold, propelled in part by economic crisis. Canada's first magnet would become its last province.

Of the country's ten provinces, Newfoundland ranks among the most exposed to the sea. Its coast is so deeply indented that, if all the notches of Labrador and the Rock were pressed straight, the resulting shoreline would extend some 12,000 miles, nearly halfway around the earth. Such exposure both blesses the region and isolates it, creating what some consider a seagirt Appalachia sequestered by its own geography and history. Geologically, in fact, the island's mountainous Great Northern Peninsula is an extension of the Appalachians. Its people are largely of English and Scotch-Irish stock—as are Appalachia's—and Irish as well. Both groups share certain qualities: independence and insularity, friendliness and industry, a love of folk music and dance, isolation from government, respect for tradition. Also, says Dr. Harris, "some 17th-century carryovers—speech patterns, styles of life, superstitions, music—are very similar between western Newfoundland and Appalachia." He often swaps folktales with Memorial University's folklorist, who grew up in the United States.

"It's astonishing," Dr. Harris adds. "I'll tell him a story that comes from a Newfoundland outport, and he'll match it with one from Appalachia that's exactly the same, except the names are different, and the seals are possums or some other animal found in Appalachia."

Both regions bind their people tightly to home—people like Alex Saunders, whom I met aboard his fishing boat at the dock in Nain, Labrador.

"Where do you belong to?" Alex asked with a grin, using the Newfoundland form for "Where are you from?" It's more than a grammatical curiosity; here one's sense of belonging, of place, runs deep. Born nearly 50 years ago in a log house in the largely Indian community of Davis Inlet, he yearned to sample the world beyond. He joined the navy, traveled some, went to university, tried life in Toronto. But as he roamed and his horizons widened, things soured. He became—in his own words—a bum.

"WHEN I CAME BACK after being away 30 years or so, it was like somebody fit a key into a slot and turned it, and it was good, y'know. This is where I live and breathe. It fills me up—the people, the land, the atmosphere, the sea, the birds, the smell of the sea, the storms, the peace, the whole shebang, eh? *Yeah.* It just feels good, y'know. *This* is where I belong."

Now in Nain, just north of Davis Inlet, Alex makes a living from Labrador's waters. Summer months he heads his boat north twice weekly to gather the catches of coastal fishermen who work from small, seasonal camps. He also fishes commercially, at least as much for pleasure as for money.

"It's a way of life," he explains. "It's a gamble, sure, every day is different. I like the independence—no one to say 'sir' to. And y'know, fishing is a disease. Once you start, you keep at it, do whatever's necessary. I jeopardize my home, all my possessions just to keep this boat going and keep fishing. People don't normally do that to earn a living. But for me, it's soul, that's what it is."

Indeed, harvesting the sea's bounty has been the area's heart and soul. Five thousand years ago, aboriginal peoples here thrived on sea mammals and fish, as have their Indian descendants and the Inuit. Basques fished and operated a whaling station in Labrador as early as 1500. The French, Spanish, West Country English, and Channel Islanders also developed seasonal fisheries.

Local fishermen still follow a sea-driven calendar, putting out salmon nets, cod traps, crab pots, and other gear according to a cycle ordained by nature. Because of decades of overfishing, however, few today make a living entirely from the sea; other work and government unemployment checks see most through the long off-season. Some pursue a more efficient way of turning fish into cash: catering to sportsmen. Excellent salmon and trout streams lace southern Labrador, and serious anglers routinely plunk down two or three thousand dollars for a week's stay at one of the area's fly-fishing camps.

Accommodations tend toward the rustic. Near Makkovik, for example, Big River Camp offers a sprawling log cabin with red leatherette sofas and rough-hewn planking, amid dark spruce forest just a few miles from the seacoast. In atmosphere it is a manly blend of clubhouse and dorm with a touch of army barrack: lights on and out at set times, meals en masse and by the clock, no fishing before 9 a.m. or after 9 p.m. No bunk beds, however. Most clients seek a modified, livable wilderness: all the necessities, some of the comforts, and none of the aggravations of home. Despite the price, guests often book years in advance for the privilege of standing hip-deep in icy streams hours on end, coping with raw drizzle and blackflies and feisty winds as they repeatedly "present" a bit of feather and fluff to a particular swatch of water—in hope that the fish they saw rise there a second ago will take the hook.

Vaughn Anthony, a salmon biologist from Maine, proudly shows me his wallet of flies. "We all tie our own—it's half the fun," he explains, generously giving me two favorites to try: a Silver Rat and a Blue Charm—"chahm" in his thick Down East accent. He also offers his personal salmon strategy.

"You get one to riise, riight? Change your fly and cahst again to the same spot. If he won't take it, change and cahst once more. Get a riise? Change again. Run it by him one more tiime and he'll hit it, *wham*. See, deciding what the fish will do, puzzling out his personality, predicting his reaction—and reacting to it—all these things are the fun of salmon fishing."

Are we dealing with the psychology of the fish or the fisherman? I ask. He smiles, suddenly silent.

Later experiences on Big River certainly proved Vaughn right about the "wham." Atlantic salmon do not sneak up to the fly. Many anglers regard them as the best game fish going, better fighters than trout, and cagey. One I hooked jumped four times, then bottomed and played dead—before racing upstream with the line. The next didn't leap, but ran in zigzags. Then I felt three quick raps on the bottom, and the line went slack. The salmon had knocked itself off Blue Chahm's hook.

NORTH OF BIG RIVER AND MAKKOVIK lies Nain, Labrador's northernmost year-round community. Beyond it are no stores, no towns, no regular transportation. But change may be in the air; northern Labrador's unspoiled nature has attracted the attention of planners and special interests. Should the land be set aside as a national park? A reserve for native peoples? Should it be developed for recreation or commerce or industry? While Canada's people and government ponder whether this land will belong to God, to Cain, or to someone else, I sample it on my own, via charter boat out of Nain.

The day dawns clear, calm, and warm—warm enough for short sleeves on deck despite the 15-knot breeze generated by the full-out throttle. Before me glides a land of many faces, all of them rocky. Geologically it belongs to the Canadian Shield, a tilted, four-billion-year-old formation that contains some of the oldest rock on the planet. Its beauty is spare and brutal: icebergs, islands of bare rock, stony elbows poking through the flimsy sweater of tundra plants. Spruce forests, a mainstay of southern Labrador, soon thin and disappear, while the terrain rises in a series of different mountain groups. First come the Kiglapaits: relatively low, coal-like in their shiny blackness, broken into jags and knife ridges that slope abruptly to the sea. Then the Kaumajet Range, an island chain of drowned peaks, reddish and sheer as mesas, but domed. Talus ringing their near-vertical walls gives the impression of buttressed castles; Labrador's aborigines considered them citadels of gods. Higher and larger loom the mountains as we plow northward, while Labrador narrows in girth, tapering toward its northernmost point at Cape Chidley. Before Chidley comes Nachvak Fiord, a wide slash amid the mile-high treeless crags and ridges of the Torngat Mountains, Labrador's most magnificent range. Jagged black striations vein sheer, deep-gray cliffs that glaciers have etched and polished. All is a jumble of abrupt hollows and peaks.

Blacks and whites dominate both the landscape and the animal life. Razorbill auks—"tinkers" to Labradoreans—flutter alongside us in a splayed V. Shaped like short and very fat cigars, these black-and-white seabirds are surprisingly agile and determined. Time and again they sidle near, flapping furiously as they skim the waves, all the while strictly keeping to their V positions. They match our speed, then gradually gain, the entire phalanx pulling ahead and veering boldly across our bow. Again and again the birds challenge us, like teenagers at a stoplight: "Hey, man, wanna drag?" Again and again, they triumph. Their exuberance seems especially welcome in this less-than-joyous realm of rock and ice, where life takes itself seriously or fails to endure.

A few miles inland from Nachvak's shore rises the province's highest peak. Known variously as Caubvick, D'Iberville, and L1, it stands somewhere between 5,320 and 5,464 feet. One route to its summit follows the braided McCormick River, rock strewn and gin clear, past bouldered terraces and talus undraped by soil, each stone resplendent as a classic nude. On one natural bench scattered boulders of fairly uniform size form a primeval Stonehenge. Farther on sits a mountain of gneiss, shot through with blood-red garnets—some as big around as a man's forearm. There are tarns as well, one an incredible sapphire color wreathed in diamond-like ice. L1's final approach frays into cracked minarets and teeter-totter talus; boulders shift underfoot, threatening to pin a leg or snap it like a toothpick. The minarets end at the edge of a cloud-filled abyss. At last, the summit! But the clouds soon dissipate, revealing the "summit" to be false. Ahead stands the real L1 peak, now visible, promising unsurpassed views of the Atlantic, of Quebec, and of Nachvak itself.

Back at sea level, I stroll a narrow beach of cobbles beside Nachvak's rippled, slaty surface. Behind me dark steeps thrust skyward. Across the fjord an even higher, fiercer wall erupts in broken summits and hanging valleys. Explorer Jacques Cartier was right—Labrador *is* rocky and forbidding. But perhaps he'd have been more upbeat if he'd brought along a hook and line when he passed by in 1534, or at least taken a cursory look ashore, before rushing off to sing the praises of southern Quebec. Look at the jagged Torngat Mountains now—the westering sun has begun to toast some color into this grand, empty bleakness. Three caribou have ventured to my beach, and I have another companion: a foot-long arctic char, just brought in on the day's third cast. It is a gorgeous fish, speckled flanks banded with iridescent pink and green that will fade all too soon. Prospects for dinner have brightened considerably, for though char do not battle like salmon, their pink flesh is more delicate than salmon's, more flavorful than trout's.

A FEW MORE FLICKS OF THE ROD and I sense with unsettling certainty that I am being watched. Not ten yards from shore rises a seal's sleek head, its wide eyes taking in my every move. Seconds later and no farther away, a 20-foot-long minke whale suddenly gasps as it breaks the surface to blow and inhale. Again and again it blows, cruising the fjord edge, then vanishing as abruptly as it appeared. There are other sounds as well: A faint roll of thunder announces the bounding course of an unseen chunk of rock, freshly broken loose from a mountain wall. Caribou ankles click softly as the animals browse the McCormick River's nearby delta; falcons "keeeer" and soar overhead. Skim ice breaks up before a rising breeze, spawning a wind chime-like clatter. Yes, the Torngats are a place of bare rock. And of magic, too.

The next day I chance upon a polar bear perched on a seaside boulder as it gnaws some kelp left by the tide. Its coat appears in good shape, though hanging loosely on the young, gangly body with oversize paws. It is almost August; bears should be fat with summer's bounty. This one, initially wary of me, quickly grows bored and returns to its kelp snack.

Wild as this land seems, its wildness is something of a mirage. Stephen Loring, a University of South Carolina archaeologist I meet on my return to Nain, explains: "Everyone who comes to Labrador talks about the beauty of this country, the wilderness aspect. Canoeists and kayakers view it as pristine. But let me tell you, there's *no* place here that native people haven't been—and left marks to prove it. Maybe not on the very highest peaks. But they've been up, down, and around most of the mountains and everywhere else."

The area, indeed the entire province, has always been a crossroads for different peoples, ecosystems, even continents. Between 500 and 200 million years ago, Africa and North America met and shook hands here, then slowly went separate ways, leaving a tidbit of Africa affixed to eastern Newfoundland: the deeply indented Avalon Peninsula. Waves of glaciers have since rolled over the region, retreated, returned. Tundra and boreal forest also have come face-to-face here, each one expanding at the other's expense as borders fluctuate according to glacial and other climatic changes. So it has been with various animal populations, including human ones. Newfoundland's variety of hunting-and-gathering societies includes arctic and temperate, Inuit and Indian, archaic and contemporary. All have relied heavily on coastal resources; many subsisted primarily on sea animals. At Port au Choix on Newfoundland's western shore, excavation to build a movie theater in the 1960s turned up burial sites of an ancient culture since named Maritime Archaic. These people ranged from northern Labrador to southern Maine 5,000 to 4,000 years ago, developing toggle harpoons, warm and watertight clothing, and other technologies that helped them thrive in a rigorous realm. Bone needles, stone weapon points and tools, pendants and other art covered with red ocher and buried with the dead today are on display at the site, now a national historic park. Port au Choix is one of countless prehistoric sites in Newfoundland, many known but not excavated.

"We used to call 'em the Indian Camps," Clayton Colbourne told me, recalling childhood impressions of some moor-like bogs and low, grassy sweeps near his hometown on the tip of Newfoundland's Great Northern Peninsula. Here the Long Range that is the island's spine finally peters out in a bulb of land only a few feet above high tide. Beyond lie rocky islets and sea. There is an obvious bond to the West Country of Dorset and Cornwall: the loneliness that comes with land's end, with life at the edge where two worlds meet. The bogs, Clayton remembered, were lumpy in a strangely regular way; though well camouflaged by vegetation, they didn't look natural—not even to children.

"We could see them quite plainly, just assumed they was Indian mounds. Even played cowboys and Indians on 'em."

While grown-ups came here to harvest hay or berries, no one moved in permanently, although the area faces the sea and might seem an obvious place for expansion. "We're fishermen," Clayton explained. "The shore o'er by the mounds there is unfit for fishin' boats. It's nothin' but a rocky shallow."

And so the mounds were never dug into, built upon, or plowed under. They remained little more than a playground for generations of local cowboys and Indians. "Indian mounds" were hardly unusual in a province that had harbored so many different Indian and Inuit cultures. This embarrassment of archaeological riches—combined with a scarcity of archaeologists, as well as Newfoundland's remoteness—helped keep the mounds near Clayton's village intact. Only in 1960 did archaeologists arrive here, interview residents about potential sites, and begin turning local sod; they would find that these "Indian mounds" were neither Indian nor Inuit, but Viking.

It was a breathtaking discovery. Even today the site, named for Clayton's nearby village of L'Anse aux Meadows, remains the only substantiated Viking colony west of Greenland, proof that the Eddas, or Norse epics, were not mere fiction. Norsemen *did* voyage this far west, island-hopping from

Norway to Newfoundland without benefit of compass or astrolabe. Leif Eriksson's Vinland *was* the New World.

Excavation showed the mounds to be the remains of eight sod buildings, remarkably similar to houses built by Icelanders and Greenlanders a thousand years ago. Investigators found few personal items—a bronze cloak pin, an oil lamp, a spindle whorl, and a small whetstone—but all closely resembled artifacts from Icelandic digs. The small number may indicate that those who settled here did not rush off, but left in an orderly, planned way.

Slag deposits and about a hundred hand-forged iron rivets common to Viking ships confirm that Norsemen smelted and forged local "bog iron" into fittings and parts, probably to repair their ships. Settlers also worked the wood of local trees, perhaps not only for their own needs but also for export to Norse colonies in treeless Greenland.

The site today is not as it was; a thousand years ago, land was lower and sea higher, temperatures somewhat warmer. So the bay that Clayton now scoffs at as too shallow was not so then. The land probably yielded vegetables, also hay for Norse cattle. Streams teemed with salmon. Then as now, the site commanded access to inshore fishing grounds of Labrador and Notre Dame Bay, as well as to the Strait of Belle Isle, which leads south to New Brunswick and the Gulf of St. Lawrence. Most Viking scholars believe L'Anse aux Meadows was both a winter camp and a base of operations from which the Norse ventured south at least as far as New Brunswick. It seems clear from both site evidence and the Eddas that they intended permanent settlement.

But Vinland already had residents—aboriginal people the Eddas call *Skraelings*—whom the Norse first traded with, then ran afoul of. The natives evidently were as competent in battle as in harvesting seals, fish, and other local animals. Relations worsened between Norse and native; lives were lost. The Europeans, vastly outnumbered by a capable enemy on its home turf, packed up and sailed back east after only a few years.

*T*ODAY THE FORMER COLONY is a UNESCO world heritage site. The Viking mounds have been returned to their pre-1960 appearance, and three reconstructed sod buildings—squat, solid, made to endure—give visitors a taste of what life was like here ten centuries ago. Clayton Colbourne was one of the local men recruited to build these reconstructions, under the guidance of Norse scholars. Thick strips of peat bog were cut, dovetailed, and stacked like long bricks into a double wall flanking a gravel core, for drainage; timber posts and beams supported the heavy roofs, also of sod.

Clayton still regards the experience as "the most interesting job I ever had. It was different. Very simple—no technical work to it. You just used yer common sense."

The Norse arrayed their buildings in a gentle arc parallel to the shore and very near it, ignoring the higher ground of a natural terrace just inland. The lee of the terrace would have given better protection from the sea's brunt, and the terrace itself would have offered better overviews. But these early settlers turned their backs to the land. First and foremost, they were mariners.

Contemporary Newfoundland fishermen don't build houses back from the sea either, but right at its edge. They feel a need to be near their boats, gear, docks, the sea itself. A mere view of waves is not enough; save that for the cemetery. No matter that the shoreline soon becomes clogged with homes and sheds and landings, leaving little room for gardens that both warm a landsman's heart and put vegetables on the table; these people are farmers of the sea.

Miles south of L'Anse aux Meadows on Highway 461, miles from any village or house, isolated gardens nudge up to the pavement like exiles seeking escape. Colorful scarecrows guard the neat, carefully weeded and composted rows of onions, cabbages, carrots, and turnips. Ghost gardens without gardeners? They seem mysterious, a bit surreal out here amid miles of wild bogs and flats, but are easily explained. Soil here happens to be a bit more fertile than Newfoundland's usual issue, and once roads and pickup trucks gave locals access to such lands, they made this resource produce. The same mind-set that considers a 50-yard walk to the sea too far for a daily commute thinks nothing of traveling miles to such gardens. It's a matter of perspectives, perspectives that persist throughout the province.

In eastern Newfoundland, the outport of Bay de Verde nestles atop a natural saddle overlooking Conception Bay. It is spare, totally lacking trees and, for the moment, people, so it is without scale. The neat, pastel houses climbing the slopes like so many morning glories could belong to dolls for all I can tell. There is not much open space among them.

"You shoulda been here a few years ago," Brian Walsh, a third-generation fisherman of decidedly Irish descent, tells me when I remark on the town's compactness. "Houses were stuck on the sides of the hill. It was unbelievably congested. There was hardly room to put out a clothesline. There's not much level land, and what there is was covered over with codfish flakes, eh, racks where everybody would dry their fish. *That* was more important than where you had your house. That and where you had your boat. The house was more an afterthought. Because if you didn't get any fish and didn't have a place to dry 'em, you weren't going to need a house anyway. 'Course, nobody then had lawns or gardens. Everybody's interest was in what we were gonna get out of the ocean. That's where everything came from; nothing came from the land."

Brian, 43 years old, pursues the same livelihood followed by his father and both grandfathers. During his childhood, he recalls, fishing "was a lot more labor intensive. The whole family had to pitch in to split and salt the catch and later to spread it out to dry on the fish flakes. There was more work to putting up a catch than there was to bringing it in."

Today, fish processing plants relieve the fisherman of this burden, and Bay de Verde is roomier without its once extensive flakes. Apart from these changes, says Brian, "we fish basically the same as my father fished, following cod when they come inshore chasing capelin, then going to another type of fishery, with different gear. Next year rolls around, you do the same thing. I suppose it's timeless."

A major cog in that wheel is the capelin run. Capelin—pronounced with a long "a"—are smelt-like ocean fish less than six inches long that spawn ashore annually in incredible numbers. Their arrival is truly a thrilling event, an annual reaffirmation of nature's abundance and cyclical renewal. It occurs every June, and fishermen set traps—large walled and floored nets, moored and buoyed—in advance. They watch for capelin's early signs: whales and mobs of seabirds dining offshore.

"We just wait," explains Brian. "They come in the millions and millions. With traps, you can get 25 or 30 thousand pounds. There's no way you can sell what you catch. No way the fish plants can handle it."

Capelin that elude predators and traps turn Newfoundland's gravel beaches spongy with spawn. Many then return to the sea, though the falling tide maroons many others, leaving some shores waist-deep in fish. Up and down the coast, people collect the strandings in bushels, to fry now or to smoke or salt for later, or to fertilize their vegetable plots. Through the summer months, markets carry dried capelin, a local delicacy.

For ages, one of capelin's predators, cod, has provided food and a product that could be sold or traded for other necessities. It was a commodity that launched fortunes. Properly dried, cod's fine white flesh kept over months and thousands of miles; it was the prime goal of migratory fishermen centuries ago, and is still widely traded around the world. Newfoundlanders have fished other species as well, changing when the season was right. But inshore fishing here has always been a summer occupation, nudged aside by winter ice. In winter, men turned to inland animals or to seals—harbor, harp, and gray.

Seal was an excellent cash crop in this chronically cash-poor land. Snow-white skins of newborn harps brought the best price, and such seals could be harvested in vast numbers easily in winter, when the mothers hauled out onto the ice by the million, gave birth, and tended their helpless offspring.

Sealing took on its own aura, becoming not only a livelihood but also a rite of passage for Newfoundland males, just as whaling in centers such as Nantucket and New Bedford was for New Englanders. It also was a form of torture, and not just for seals. Men took innumerable risks in signing on, accepting ten weeks or so of bad food, filthy conditions, miserable weather, and extreme physical hardship both aboard the sealing ships and on the ice searching for newborn whitecoats. Families suffered, knowing husbands and sons and fathers were embarked on a pursuit that bore poor odds for survival. Malnutrition, frostbite, amputation, and death were hazards even into recent times.

Brian, a veteran sealer before preservation and animal rights groups halted the killing of baby harp seals in the 1970s, knew such hazards firsthand. "It was more important to go to the ice—go sealing—than to have a high school diploma," he recalls. "When you came back you were quite respected."

One season, Brian and his father worked the same sealing ship. The crew took to the ice in early morning. "It was bitter frost, probably 20 below zero, beautifully calm, and we went off following another ship's crew; 60 of us, 120 of them. We walked and walked, probably four hours. Sure enough, they were into the seals, about ten miles from the ships. So we started killing a few. All of a sudden it started to snow. And snow and snow. The master watch said, 'Boys, I think it's time we got aboard. We got about three or four hours to walk back, the wind is comin' from the southeast, so we'll have a bit of snow.'

"We started walking and walking and walking. Started to get real t'ick—you're on the ice, and the snow is white, and you can't see anything. A whiteout, no up or down. Absolutely nothing. The second mate was in charge, and he didn't even have a compass. Well, we got lost. Nobody knew where we were going. One guy had chest pains, couldn't make it. Second mate said, 'Everyone for themselves.' He was a bloody idiot."

Brian's father, however, pulled out a little compass he'd had the foresight to pack along. With that and with luck, the men found their way back to the icebound ship.

"She wasn't much to look at. But I tell you, buddy, when I got aboard her that day, you're talking home sweet home. Never stayed in a hotel as snug as that boat that night. I still can see myself in that whiteout, trying to find her. I don't know what the appeal of it was. The mystique, the adventure? Some things you do in life you forget pretty quickly. Then there's things that never fade. I'll never forget that day as long as I live, that day walking on the ice."

*L*IKE MANY NEWFOUNDLANDERS, Brian knows of life's harsher side, and not all from sealing. Of his Bay de Verde childhood, he says, "The only heat in the house was a coal stove; 11 o'clock at night when the fire'd go out, that was it; you'd go to bed. Next morning the water barrel was frozen; so was the chamber pot under your bed. Ninety percent of Newfoundland was that way. These were your 'independent' Newfoundlanders. There was no water, no sewer, no nothing. Everybody was 'independent,' all right—independently poor. Except for the merchant class.

"Some areas had caribou, partridge, ducks. But around here people were hungry half the time, and undernourished. I'd say there was more rickets, and no dental work. Every second child you'd meet had his teeth falling out of his head. *Every* adult. We had plenty of flour, peas, beans, and potatoes. But that was it. In the morning my father would go to what we jokingly referred to as 'the woods' here. He'd cut sticks four or five feet high—all there was—and spend the day hauling them home on a hand slide to warm the house."

Like many rural folk, Newfoundlanders eased rough times and celebrated happy ones with a homegrown music they developed, relying mainly on guitar, fiddle, and accordion. Its roots go back to English, Scottish, and Irish ballads and jigs, and of late it has worn the overprint of country and western. Not even rock and roll has drowned out the sound.

*M*USICIANS LIKE JIM PAYNE have succeeded in swimming against the current of a larger world. Jim "started singing about the same time I started talking. When I was a teenager I wanted to be a rock and roll star. I still listen to all kinds of music. But I've always come back to Newfoundland stuff. I believe in the living tradition. Music is part of what makes us Newfoundlanders. It's part of what keeps us together. Family reunions and parties always have storytelling and singing; there's a sense of belonging. Music helps Newfoundlanders relate to each other when they live in other parts of the country. It's our connection to home."

Jim adds a telling note about his fans, particularly the older generation: "They won't say, 'You're a great singer, boy. You've got a beautiful voice.' They say, 'You're a great singer, boy. I can understand every word you say.' That's their greatest compliment. All these songs have stories to them, and if they can't understand the lyrics, what's the point of listening?"

Patrick O'Flaherty, the writer, reflected on his homeland one day in St. John's. "Life has been hard here. Let no one sentimentalize it—Newfoundland is a very physical place. Its population is stagnant or in decline. The climate is awful, the land is rocky, resources are scarce. Our best industry is fishing and it's *never* been good. We've had very few periods of prosperity; our economy has always been down or trembling on the edge.

"But what strikes me is the continuity of life here. The place endures. It's resilient, like a barnacle on a rock. It's really hard for people to leave. It exerts an attraction, and I think it'll stay that way, like Scotland. The Scots are part of Great Britain, you know, but they're absolutely distinctive. Their culture endures. Their accent is completely different, their thinking is completely different, their way of building things is completely different. Newfoundland is like that. And I think it has a similar destiny, to be a kind of separate, distinctive, quasi-country on the fringe of North America. It's an unusual place, a queer old spot."

Explosive surf near Flat Rock fails to rouse harp seals sunning ■
atop pack ice in early spring. Soon the seals will mate, then head for
their summering grounds in lands north of the Arctic Circle.

■ *Living proof of Labrador's cultural diversity, the Moravian church string ensemble in Nain features Inuit musicians (opposite). The church, founded by Germans in 1771, also has a choir and a brass band—its instruments felt-wrapped to ward off frostbite during outdoor performances. Once living in the nomadic way of the Inuit, Nancy Pamak (above) now leads a more sedentary life in Nain, where she raises houseplants "to bring outdoor smells inside." Her adopted town (left)— largest and most northerly of Labrador's coastal communities—links a sparsely settled south with a wild, barren northland.*

Too close for comfort, an encroaching iceberg prompts fishermen near Cut Throat Island to haul in nets before the jagged intruder destroys them. Fishing season is mainly June and July, as salmon and char enter streams to spawn. Seals and polar bears hungering for the same bounty shred many a net. Other challenges of fishing include harsh weather and the unvarnished life of seasonal camps. Rewards also exist: clean water and air, a wildness that nurtures Inuit values and a sense of belonging, of place.

■ *Chiseled walls of Western Brook Pond (opposite) testify to the past power of moving ice and water. Ancient glaciers and streams gouged a landlocked trough, sometimes called an inland fjord, into the barren plateau. Over time, precipitation and mountain streams transformed the gorge into a freshwater lake. Today, local strains of salmon and char thrive here, joined every summer by tour boats (above) in this major attraction of the 697-square-mile Gros Morne National Park. Named for the Island of Newfoundland's highest mountain, which rises to 2,633 feet, Gros Morne possesses unsurpassed scenic and geological features that led to its designation as a UNESCO world heritage site in 1987.*

■ *Avalanche of homes all but overflows François, a classic Newfoundland outport pinned between fjord-like walls and the sea. Lacking forests, farms, and even roads, the village depends on a biweekly ferry for nearly all supplies. Fishing has sustained François for more than 200 years. Residents fill idle hours with*

*homegrown pastimes—music,
conversation, dance (opposite).
The cats in repose at right seem
to embody the outport's relatively
slow-paced style of life.*

FOLLOWING PAGES: Ruddy sunset ■
*afterglow backlights islands and
burnishes waters in southern
Newfoundland's Hermitage Bay.*

■ Treading waters known to
16th-century pinnaces and men-
of-war, a modern containership
plows the narrows (left) that link
the Atlantic to St. John's small
but well-protected port. The
Romanesque Basilica of St.
John the Baptist and a rusty
Soviet trawler (above) flank the
colorful downtown of a city that
serves as the province's political,
economic, and intellectual
hub— and as home to a fifth of
its nearly 600,000 people.

FOLLOWING PAGES: Plain ■
clapboard houses, haunting
vistas, and time-honored ways
endure on Change Island.

TIM THOMPSON

■ *Summer's here! Come August, a plank becomes a diving board for Musgrave Harbour youngsters, despite frigid waters and a 20-mile-an-hour "breeze."*

■ *Down the coast at Bay de Verde, crews of future fishermen roughhouse aboard their fathers' boats, pursuing traditional play that also hones skills they will need in adult life.*

■ *Faced with few anchorages and a rock palisade for a wharf, Pouch Cove fishermen haul out*

onto ramp-like landing stages, perch their shanties on stilts, and commute by ladder.

■ *Black-and-white and wary, immature kittiwakes (opposite) wait for a parent to bring a fishy morsel to their cliffside abode in Witless Bay Bird Sanctuary. Tens of thousands of northern gannets crowd a lone sea stack at Cape St. Mary's (above), the continent's second largest gannetry, after Quebec's Bonaventure Island. Endlessly they perform, rising in a living cloud over the rock, then soaring off singly, plummeting to the sea, and returning to the "cloud" before they choose a landing site, deliver their cargo of fish, and take off again.*

FOLLOWING PAGES: Rising moon outshines ■
a Trinity Bay beacon. In five centuries,
Newfoundland's stern coasts and blinding storms
have claimed more than 7,000 ships.

The Historic

■ *Atlantic waves wash granite boulders below the lighthouse at Peggy's Cove, in Nova Scotia.*

Maritimes

By Gene S. Stuart
Photographs by James P. Blair

For generations, the familiar landmark and its beacon have guided village fishermen home.

51

*I*N THE SHADOW OF A FOREST scented with ever-greens and edged with dawn, I watched a cold coastal landscape transform as if an unfinished earth sought balance and repose. Shapes seemed to alter, disappear, form again. Slowly, gracefully, nature draped spruce and fir trees in glistening moisture, shrouded the rocky shoreline in swirling fog, covered soft mountain contours in descending clouds. Rocks appeared to dissolve in air, trees to rise from vapor. In the silence that gripped that mystical, evolving world, I moved beyond the shore and walked on the bottom of the sea.

I followed the ebbing tide far out onto the Bay of Fundy's rubble-strewn floor. When I looked back, the fog had lifted, and the forest and mountains seemed small. Alma, New Brunswick, a fishing village built at water's edge, now stood far inland. Moored boats foundered in mud. The scene created the illusion that the living earth had drawn a breath, lifting the land above the sea. Twice daily the sea withdraws, and the land appears to rise; twice daily the sea returns, and the land seems to subside with a sigh. In the upper bay, the difference between high and low water may be as much as 50 feet. This is the rhythm of Fundy—site of the world's greatest range of tides.

Scientists tell this epic story of the bay's creation: More than 400 million years ago, long before earth's land assumed forms now familiar, tectonic plates bearing two continents drifted on courses of certain collision. Their gradual but violent meeting thrust up a rugged mountain range; we call its ancient, worn remains the Appalachians. About 200 million years ago, massive fractures split the earth's crust in a rifting process that broke apart the continents and created the Atlantic Ocean. One of the rifts associated with this breakup eventually became a valley. When sea levels began to rise just after the last ice age, about 14,000 years ago, Atlantic waters surged into the valley, drowning it. We call this ancient, drowned valley the Bay of Fundy.

At high tide some 24 cubic miles of water flow into the 170-mile-long bay—a volume equal to the daily discharge of all the world's rivers. The bay

■ *Ebb tide strands fishing boats in Nova Scotia's
Sandy Cove near the Bay of Fundy, where daily tidal
variations average more than 20 feet.*

begins to narrow past its mouth, compressing the incoming tide to greater and greater heights as it moves toward the head of the bay. The length and funnel shape of the bay are such that the falling tide sweeps out into the ocean just as the rising tide begins to push back in. This creates resonance, which gives Fundy the swaying rhythm necessary for gigantic tides.

An older explanation of the creation of the bay and its phenomenal tides comes from the mythology of the Micmac, native people who once lived along Fundy's shores. According to Micmac stories told in song, the giant Glooscap was taking a bath one day in a trench dug for him by Beaver. His friend Whale swam in and refused to leave until Glooscap walked to shore. Glooscap got up and Whale swam away with such turbulent splashing that the waters slosh back and forth to this day.

Arms of the Atlantic—bays, straits, and gulfs—embrace the incredible coasts of New Brunswick, Prince Edward Island, and Nova Scotia, the provinces of Canada known as the Maritimes. In New Brunswick, part of the mainland, the northern Appalachians run to the Gulf of St. Lawrence and plunge beneath the water, then rise again as part of Newfoundland. Narrow marshland anchors mainland Nova Scotia to New Brunswick, and water surrounds its other part, Cape Breton Island, as well as Prince Edward Island.

*N*O ONE KNOWS which Europeans first reached these shores or when they came. They might have been Viking adventurers of the Dark Ages (a runic stone found in Nova Scotia attests to a Viking visit). Or perhaps the first were hardy Basques who fished far afield; or Breton fishermen who settled for a season and named the island, or only paused there to repair their nets and salt their catch of cod before returning home.

Tradition says that John Cabot landed on Cape Breton Island in 1497 during his explorations for England. There, in the shadow of Sugarloaf Mountain, he refilled his water casks from a tumbling stream. Giovanni da Verrazano explored the region in 1524 and claimed it for France. In 1534 Jacques Cartier made the first of his three voyages on behalf of the French king, Francis I. On July 1 he sailed along the coast of Prince Edward Island, landing in four places to see the sweet-smelling trees that grew there.

Verrazano was probably the first to call a part of the New World Acadia. Its beauty and richness reminded him of tales of Arcadia, a region of ancient Greece celebrated by poets as a pastoral paradise. This new earthly paradise, Acadia, came to include what are now the Maritimes and northern New England, and French settlers there were known as Acadians. In 1605, on the bay we call Fundy, the French established a presence in the New World with the settlement of Port-Royal; its mainstay was the fur trade with the Indians.

Port-Royal stood on Nova Scotia's Annapolis Basin and edged the

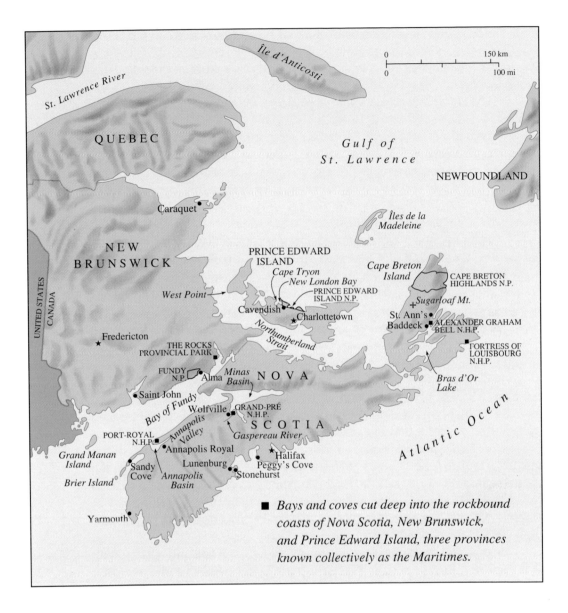

■ Bays and coves cut deep into the rockbound
coasts of Nova Scotia, New Brunswick,
and Prince Edward Island, three provinces
known collectively as the Maritimes.

Annapolis Valley, Nova Scotia's most productive agricultural land. The bay
and streams were alive with fish; the dense timberland was rich with game. The
settlers, all men, ranged from nobles to peasants and included the explorer
Samuel de Champlain. They constructed a group of buildings they called The
Habitation, basing its plan on those of 16th-century manors in Normandy.

A reconstruction of The Habitation is now a national historic site.
There a young guide, outfitted in the wooden shoes, full-cut shirt, and blousy
breeches of the period, greeted me in English with a heavy French accent. I
passed through studded oak doors and back in time to a new colony in a new

land. The buildings surround a courtyard and range from chapel to kitchen to blacksmith shop. Officials and other gentlemen had modestly furnished private quarters. I climbed dark stairs to the upper floor, where wooden shoes and thin pallets in large rooms reflected the communal life of peasants.

The Habitation's cozy atmosphere belies a history of hardship. But despite sickness and severe winters, the French made every effort to bring *joie de vivre* to Acadia. In November 1606, lawyer and poet Marc Lescarbot arranged a surprise for Champlain and others when they returned from a voyage of exploration. Surprise must have been the least of it. As the travelers' ships hove into view, costumed colonists and Indians in canoes began the first performance of *Le Théâtre de Neptune en la Nouvelle-France,* a play in verse that Lescarbot had written as "some piece of merriment" for the occasion.

Champlain and Lescarbot organized a club called *L'Ordre de Bons Temps,* The Order of Good Cheer, as a diversion during the winter of 1606–07. Some 15 members, all gentlemen, took turns as chief steward for a day, each seeking to improve upon the menu of the others. Great pomp and ceremony surrounded these occasions. The steward, with the chain of office around his neck, a napkin draped on his shoulder, and an official staff in his hand, led members in procession from the kitchen. Each bore a different dish to the long table set with gleaming pewter before a great stone fireplace. Membertou, a distinguished Micmac chief more than a hundred years old (so old that he could recall Cartier's 1534 voyage), held a place of honor at the banquets. Lescarbot observed that "whatever our gourmands at home may think, we found as good cheer at Port-Royal as they in Paris and at a cheaper rate."

Despite daily feasts, illness took its toll; despite peace with the Indians, squabbles in Europe over rights to the colony sealed Port-Royal's fate. On the strength of Cabot's explorations, England claimed all lands north of Florida. In November 1613 an expedition from Jamestown, in the young English colony of Virginia, looted and burned Port-Royal, and the French and British struggle for supremacy in the region began in earnest.

Reestablished some five miles away, Port-Royal became "the football of the nations" in intermittent war. British, French, or Indian forces besieged the citadel 14 times, and it changed hands 7 times. With British conquest in 1710, Port-Royal became Annapolis Royal. In 1713 a treaty gave mainland Nova Scotia to the British; the French kept Cape Breton Island.

While nations struggled, Acadian families farmed, pleading neutrality during the years of British conquest. By 1750, about 10,000 Acadians lived around the Bay of Fundy, more than 1,300 of them in the village of Grand-Pré—Great Meadow or Marsh—in the Annapolis Valley beside the Minas Basin. Grand-Pré was the heart of Acadia and home to Longfellow's tragic heroine, Evangeline, "the pride of the village."

Over thousands of years, tides have built thick deposits of silt along the broad Minas shore. As early as the 1630s, Acadian settlers eagerly exploited this gift of nature, constructing dikes and *aboiteaux,* sluices with gates that allow fresh water to flow out, but keep salty tides from coming in. By 1755, Acadians had transformed 12,600 acres of muddy bay bottom and tidal marsh into rich farmland, changing the configuration of the shore.

The contrast between land and sea is astounding when viewed from the top of a Grand-Pré dike. With Ross Friars, manager of the Wolfville Tourist Bureau, I stood on a dike at low tide, when the withdrawn sea had left contoured mud flats shimmering in morning sunlight. Behind the dike, fields (many of them below sea level) grew thick with alfalfa and wheat, and pastureland stretched to a rise where orchards marked the original shore, just as they had in Acadian times. "This land has always provided its owners with a stable economy," said Ross. "About 70 percent of the crops grown in Nova Scotia come from this valley. Even in the Great Depression no one went hungry here."

*A*CADIANS WANTED little more than to be left alone. Shunning conflict, they quickly developed a close-knit society. Historian François-Edmé Rameau de Saint-Père wrote that they "enjoyed simple domestic pleasures as well as violent horse races and adventurous fishing expeditions. They liked the activity of church feast days, the processions and the solemn hymn singing that seemed to mingle with the ocean's beat. At parties, old French songs would be heard as well as recitals of hunting experiences and pirate sagas. At other times, solitary thinkers that they were, they felt in tune with the melancholy of the sea. . . . They created legends and folk songs. . . ."

"I'll take you to a place few outsiders know," Ross said, and we drove to a spot (now a dairy farm) where the Gaspereau River stretches to the bay. There, in 1755, the British sent the Acadians of Grand-Pré into exile on an ebbing tide after torching village and fields. According to a tale passed down through generations, the British loaded the village church bell onto a ship that sank in a storm; it can still be heard tolling beneath the waves.

"I come to this place often," said Ross. "It's so peaceful." And it was beautiful. We lingered, as if expecting a glimpse of departing sails. Holsteins arranged themselves in a row behind us, their bovine stares matching our melancholy gaze, their jaws working in pensive unison as they chewed their cuds.

After Grand-Pré was destroyed, some Acadians in New Brunswick and mainland Nova Scotia went into hiding; many fled to French-held Quebec or Cape Breton. Expulsions sent others as far away as Europe. Later, some Acadians found refuge in Louisiana. In peaceful times, many returned to Nova Scotia and New Brunswick, where they resumed farming and fishing. Today, more than one-third of the people of New Brunswick are of Acadian descent.

The French, in 1719, had begun fortifying Louisbourg, a town in Cape Breton on an eastern bay that gives onto the Atlantic. The fortress was one of the largest ever built in the New World by a European power. The story goes that as expenses for the construction escalated and praises for Louisbourg soared, King Louis XV went to a window in Versailles and joked that the fortress was so enormous he would surely see its towers rising above the horizon. British capture of Louisbourg came in 1758, when the town had 4,000 permanent residents. British engineers leveled Louisbourg; modern scholarship has helped to reconstruct one-fifth of it. Today Louisbourg is the largest historical reconstruction in North America and is preserved as a national historic park.

On a midsummer day, a glittering silver bay stretched beneath a pewter sky. A cold, damp wind swept the land with the odor of dried cod. I clattered across a drawbridge toward the Dauphin Gate, the main landward approach to the fortress. A sentry in an 18th-century uniform suddenly swung his musket toward me and spoke abruptly in French.

"Halt!" I think he said. So I did. He shouted an alarm to a sentry posted within the gate. The bilingual interrogation that followed identified me as an American, but I was allowed to "proceed in peace and approach." A couple walking nearby were questioned further, for they looked suspiciously British—both wore red jackets.

Military structures—bastions, barracks, a powder magazine—recall one purpose of the fortress: protection of the Gulf of St. Lawrence and New France. Louisbourg also served as a center of trade between France, the West Indies, Canada, and New England. Storehouses and merchants' well-appointed dwellings revealed a middle class made prosperous by trade. More modest buildings were used by the fishing industry that supplied France with cod. I watched a man fillet cod and lay it out on flakes, or drying platforms. In the old days, several thousand migrant fishermen and shore workers could produce 15 million pounds of dried cod and 1,500 barrels of cod-liver oil in a summer. I imagined the harbor dense with a forest of masts that seemed to grow from the bay—masts of fishing boats, merchantmen, and warships.

The day lengthened and grew colder, and I stopped at the King's Bakery for a loaf of whole-wheat-and-rye bread fresh from the oven. It was a soldier's daily ration—a pound and a half—round, toasty, and comforting to hold. I ate this delicious hand warmer as I strolled slippery cobbled streets. I chatted with a kitchen maid in cap and apron who tended a sputtering roast over an open fire; watched the changing of the guard; and visited the damp, bleak prison. In the window of a crowded tavern, glowing candlelight wavered invitingly through panes of uneven glass.

Northwest of Louisbourg, the Cape Breton highlands rise in undulating hills and mountains reminiscent of the Scottish Highlands—and evocative of the province's Scottish heritage. In 1621, King James VI of Scotland (who ruled Great Britain as James I) granted poet Sir William Alexander lands establishing New Scotland. The charter, in Latin, gave Nova Scotia its name, but Scots did not settle there in large numbers until the late 1700s.

"Scottish tradition here in Cape Breton is second to none except in Scotland itself," faculty member Hugh Higgins commented as I followed his robust, kilted form through the Hall of the Clans at the Gaelic College of Celtic Arts and Crafts in St. Ann's. The hall celebrates Scottish history; the college preserves Scottish culture.

"I believe we are the stronghold of Scottish culture in this country," said executive director Jim MacAulay. "We're trying to get people conversing in Gaelic again. The language has probably retained greater purity in Cape Breton than it has in Scotland because of our relative isolation. We have fewer 'borrow' words. There, more 'loaner' words come in with high tech industries electronic media and the oil fields in the North Sea. There are advantages to not being industrialized," he laughed. "In any house you enter in St. Ann's and in rural communities north of here, you'll find Gaelic speakers."

I FOUND GAELIC SPEAKERS, young ones, in the college's classes for children, all of whom wore kilts. In one room, a boy about seven years old, alone with his tutor, rolled the melodious language on his tongue. In another, youngsters flung themselves into highland dances. Tootles and squeaks lured me to piping classes. Elsewhere, a weaver bent to the rhythm of her loom, on which a tartan was taking shape, and fledgling fiddlers rendered timeless tunes.

"A lot of tales are in the form of song," Jim said. "People didn't tend to write history; instead, it was passed from parents to children in song and kept pretty accurate over many generations in Scotland and in Cape Breton. You have a few bards in each community, and they'll make up a song about a wedding, or building a new barn, or something funny that someone has done. You hear people around here singing of events that happened 200 years ago or more with an accuracy of detail that makes them as vivid as when they occurred.

"We often have a milling frolic. In Scotland they call it 'waulking the tweed.' When weavers finish cloth, it must be laid out on a long table and treated to make it set and tighten up right nice. This is a bit of an arduous task, so to make it easier, they sing songs. At a recent frolic we ate herring and potatoes, common fare of the early Scots here because of the abundance of herring in the bay and the ease of growing potatoes. Frolics help keep the folklore alive."

The bay Jim spoke of is St. Ann's. It parallels a channel connecting the Atlantic with Bras d'Or Lake, an inland sea where subtle tides rise and fall sometimes scant inches, sometimes imperceptibly, like an addition of mist to ocean, a decrease of breath from air. Some 50 miles long and 20 miles across at its widest point, the lake adds about 600 miles to Nova Scotia's coastline.

More than a century ago, Scottish-born Alexander Graham Bell sailed these scenic waters and determined that he would make his summer home near the village of Baddeck. Bell's experiments in sound and his invention of the telephone are well known, but he also excelled in aerodynamics, and Baddeck Bay was the site of many firsts. There, in 1909, *Silver Dart,* built by Bell's Aerial Experiment Association, made the first powered flight in Canada; it used the frozen bay as a landing strip. There, in 1919, Bell's huge hydrofoil, HD-4, set a world water speed record of 70.86 miles per hour. On the shore, Bell joined more than 3,000 tetrahedral cells to make kites more than 40 feet long, and he often sat in a tetrahedral shelter to watch them fly.

The Alexander Graham Bell National Historic Park at Baddeck displays the astonishing range of the inventor's genius. The park staff introduces children to Bell's world through kite-making classes for youngsters six and older, a qualification I more than met. My classmates and I sprawled on the floor with plastic, wood, and tape to create uniform aerodynamic miracles. Final touches with marking pens made each kite distinctive. Mine bore the National Geographic's rectangular logo and the label "Canada's Incredible Kite."

I conceded the joy of kite flying to the children. On a breezy mountaintop, I watched with other adults as youngsters ran, leaped, fell down slopes, and stumbled up inclines, each holding a kite aloft until that thrilling moment when it became airborne. More than an hour later I passed that way again. Three boys still stood on a grassy knoll silently tugging their kite strings, enraptured by the discovery that their creations could capture the wind.

*H*ARDY, INDUSTRIOUS SCOTS, as well as Acadian, Irish, and English immigrants, settled Prince Edward Island. Some have likened its shape to a canoe floating in the Gulf of St. Lawrence just off the coasts of New Brunswick and Nova Scotia. Micmac legend says the Creator fashioned the island from red clay, dressed it in forests and flowers, and bade the giant Glooscap fly with it to the most peaceful place on earth. Whale showed him the way, and spouted great columns of water when they reached the spot most pleasing to the Creator.

Prince Edward Island, or PEI, consists largely of sedimentary materials deposited in a shallow sea more than 250 million years ago. Measuring 140 miles long and from 4 to 40 miles wide, it is the smallest of Canada's provinces. With some 128,000 residents, it is also the least populous. Ironically, it is both the most densely populated province and the most rural—in the 1980s, scarcely more than a third of the people lived in towns. Little of the old forest admired by Cartier remains. Cultivated fields, dairy farms, and pasturelands quilt the island in a patchwork of red and green. Roads, usually straight and running parallel, stitch the island in diagonal patterns that follow old survey lines.

"What is striking to me is that the land here is so different from New Brunswick, Nova Scotia, and Newfoundland. It is so much more gentle," said John Cousins. A history teacher and folklorist, John lives on a farm at the western end of the island. "And not only is the land flat and gentle, but the sea in comparison is gentle also. It's gentle in the meeting with the land. In places you can walk way out into the water. I have an idea that this may have influenced the personalities of the people. Prince Edward Islanders tend to be gentle people. There are many different groups, and we've lived together with little clashing between us. Oh, we sometimes complain, and we're great people to gossip, but there's been no violent upheaval.

"Socially and economically, the southern Appalachians and PEI have a great deal in common. Both had English and Scottish settlers, and today we have their old stories and ballads. Many British ballads have died in North America except in North Carolina and in the Maritimes and Newfoundland, where you find the same ones—cultural survivals. Life on the island has been farming, it's been fishing, and until the last generation the old parts of the culture, the oral traditions, survived. In the long winters there would be ten-foot snowdrifts, but people traveled by horse and sleigh and visited to the wee hours of the morning, singing songs and telling stories—funny stories, or tales of ghosts, witches, fairies, and the devil. Storytelling is a dying art. This end of the island didn't get electricity until the late 1950s. Once television came, it wrecked ghost stories and good conversation. Now hour-long folktales are replaced by afternoon soaps. Having grown up with tales hundreds of years old, I regret that. I love to get together with people and tell tall tales."

The most noted storyteller of PEI told tales in the form of books. Lucy Maud Montgomery, of Cavendish, wrote *Anne of Green Gables* and 19 other novels. Prince Edward Island National Park includes a house, now restored as Green Gables, that belonged to Maud Montgomery's cousins. Each year some 300,000 "Anne" enthusiasts make pilgrimages to this shrine of make-believe.

Trailing Japanese parents and their two little girls, I visited the house and adjacent hollows, brooks, and forest where the fictional orphan lived. The girls clutched copies of an "Anne" novel in Japanese and squealed in recognition of places mentioned in the beloved books. On the Haunted Woods Trail, I paused before a plaque bearing Maud Montgomery's words: "I had in my vivid imagination a passport to the geography of fairyland."

The geography of PEI invariably leads you to the sea. Anne's fictional adoptive family were coastal farmers. John Cousins grew up on the coast; his father was a fisherman. "But he traveled to New Brunswick in the wintertime to work in the lumber woods," John said. "Lumbermen walked into camps and stayed for four months. They entertained each other. There would be two or three good singers; maybe someone played the fiddle. My father couldn't carry a tune, but he could recite. And that was his job—he recited poems."

John played his guitar and sang of Peter Emberly, an island boy who went to the lumber woods more than a hundred years ago and never returned. "That song was not written down, but it spread through Maine to the American Midwest," John explained. Another island song tells of the *Gracie M. Parker,* a schooner laden with lumber that struggled in a gale at Christmastime and sank.

In the Maritimes, the story of ships, storms, and perilous coasts is as old as the earliest settlements. Once, open-fire beacons may have been used to signal vessels at sea. Canada's first lighthouse, a stone tower built in 1733, guided ships into Louisbourg Harbour. In Canada today, some 20,000 lighthouses, buoys, beacons, and other navigational aids warn of ironhard coasts, shape-shifting islands, treacherous reefs, and changeable currents. But old lighthouses, like sailing ships, are a vanishing species.

West Point Lighthouse, at the western end of PEI, sits only a dune away from the Northumberland Strait. On a clear day the shores of New Brunswick shimmer in the distance. Towering 85 feet, the lighthouse is among the island's tallest. It first flashed its lightning-bright beacon (fueled by cod-liver oil) in 1876. William MacDonald tended that light and continued as keeper for 50 years. "Everyone called him Lighthouse Willie. He was my great-grandfather," Carol Livingstone told me as we sat in the restored lighthouse parlor. Lighthouse Willie's grizzled and windblown countenance gazed out from an old photograph. "He and his family lived here in summer and on their nearby farm in winter when the lighthouse didn't operate—the strait is frozen solid from December until April or May. This was a farming and fishing community, and the lighthouse was a center people would come to."

Electricity and automation in 1963 eliminated the need for a keeper. Empty, the lighthouse suffered neglect. In 1982 Carol and other local women set out to restore it. "We wanted to capture an atmosphere: my great-grandparents' house," Carol said. "When we opened in 1984, you could see this building alive again." Women make up the staff. Most of them are Lighthouse Willie's descendants, and most of them have his wife's red hair, bright as a beacon. Locals gather at the lighthouse restaurant for camaraderie and for lobster chowder (Carol's mother's recipe) as thick as pudding. Lighthouse rooms and a new wing decorated in 19th-century style draw guests from "away," as islanders refer to the rest of the world.

I spent several days at West Point strolling the sands along the strait, talking with fishermen and their families, and driving coastal roads where pastures and fields run to the edge of russet cliffs. At night I climbed narrow lighthouse stairs to a narrow bedroom above the parlor where a quilt stitched from satin and brocade scraps brightened an iron bed. One evening, as a storm approached, radios warned fishermen to make for shelter. That night the old tower shuddered in the winds of a tempest as unstoppable as a tide.

In the parlor Carol pointed to an oil chandelier. "My grandmother would light it, then tell us stories." Carol told me of a shipwreck during the lighthouse's first year. "A sailing ship from Europe went aground on the reef here, and the sailors had to stay for the winter."

John Cousins had told me of a phantom ship seen by islanders. I asked Carol if it appears near West Point. "I guess it does!" she said. "Some people see it only in August. My sisters and I saw it in March three years ago. There were lights along the shore. We knew they were too close to be in New Brunswick, and it couldn't have been a ship, not in winter, so we stopped the car. Two tall masts looked to be in flames. Now, some people say they can see the crew jumping overboard, hear their shouts. I can't say that, but I can say we saw two tall, burning masts, and the strait was frozen solid. We drove to a hill for a better view, but fog rolled in and the ship disappeared."

*N*EAR WEST POINT, I joined tall, suntanned Robert Ellsworth and a small crew in a fishing boat, the *Julie E.* Stark red cliffs loomed larger than they did from landward as we bobbed near other boats, watching men fish—for moss.

In clear, shallow water, stands of Irish moss grew like miniature forests, their fronds waving in the liquid breezes of gentle currents. Men drove boats back and forth as if they were harvesting machines in a field, pulling the crop from the rocky seafloor with wide, curved rakes. The seaweed is used commercially as a thickening agent in products ranging from toothpaste to powdered milk and dog food.

"Some boats haul in 7,000 pounds or more a day," said Robert. "Irish moss is pretty good money. On a good day you can make about 600 dollars. But I like fishing better than mossing."

Robert started the engine occasionally to move the boat away from reefs. Since fishing crews keep constant watch for boats in distress, our random drifting caused concern. The radio crackled, and a distant voice shouted, "Robert! Are you in there, Robert?"

"There's a woman here from away," Robert yelled, "and we're showing her around. We're sailing, just sailing." He turned on the engine and "sailed" us to deeper water. "We start on the first of May fishing scallops, then herring and mackerel," he told me. "Then we fish lobsters until the tenth of October. They're the best money."

The surface nearby began trembling with a hissing sound, and fluttering shards of silver glistened in the sunlight. We came around, stopped, and drifted. "Mackerel! The first school we've seen this year," said Robert. "Hear them snapping? They're playing around. There's a few mackerel in that. You'll pick up six or seven thousand pounds over there. The last part of July and the first part of August you see big schools—acres and acres of them. With my brother in his boat, we circle a school and catch them with seine nets."

Another voice shouted through static: "Are you in there, Robert? You all right, Robert?"

"Just watching a school of mackerel," he answered.

While lumbering, farming, mining, and manufacturing have been important in the Maritimes, fishing and the sea have been their essence. In 1990 the three provinces had some 10,000 registered fishing vessels. That year, the great commercial ports of Saint John, in New Brunswick, and Halifax, in Nova Scotia, handled cargoes totaling nearly 31 million tons, and ferries transported more than 3 million people. Many came by ferry from New England, famed for a shipbuilding tradition that influenced Maritime history.

After the Acadians were driven from Nova Scotia in the 1750s, New Englanders settled the land they had farmed. During and after the American Revolution, many New Englanders, loyal to the crown, immigrated to New Brunswick. They went to Nova Scotia by the thousand, doubling the province's population in the 1780s. Lunenburg was settled by Germans, Swiss, and French Huguenots. Lunenburg, Yarmouth, also in Nova Scotia, and Saint John were just a few of the Maritime shipbuilding towns. By the mid-1800s, these centers ranked among the largest in the New World.

"The masts of Lord Nelson's ship, *Victory,* at Trafalgar were New Brunswick spruce, I am told," said Mitchell Franklin, a New Brunswick businessman who lives near the Bay of Fundy. I stood with Mitchell on a bayside cliff. Far below, stumps of tall poles and a rotted wharf rose above a tidal creek that runs into the bay. "That was Tynemouth, one of the largest shipbuilding communities," he said. "Between 300 and 500 men lived and worked there. Some of the greatest wooden ships were built along these shores, and they sailed the world."

*A*BOUT 1700, SHIPWRIGHTS in New England had begun constructing sleek wooden craft called schooners. Historian Christopher Moore writes that they were designed "to run the obstacle courses of the North American coasts, to weave easily through treacherous inshore passages, and to speed over the distances between isolated coastal ports." Most famous of Canadian schooners was the *Bluenose,* and her story is one that Nova Scotians especially never tire of repeating. The two-masted fishing schooner was the fastest deep-water sailing ship of her class and became a legend for never relinquishing the International Fishermen's Trophy over an 18-year period of racing competition. Canada has honored the ship by showing her on stamps and ten-cent pieces. The *Bluenose* was built in 1921 at Lunenburg and first sailed from there. I first set sail from Lunenburg also—on the *Bluenose II.*

The schooner, a copy of her predecessor, moved away from her berth under diesel power and turned into the long harbor. There the engines stopped, sails were hoisted, and canvas snapped and swelled as it caught the breeze. The most amazing impression of my first sailing experience was the palpable silence. Not a mast or a plank creaked as we ran before the wind. Sails curved taut to the wind without a sound. Ahead, a forbidding bank of fog closed the bay's entrance to the open Atlantic like a barrier to another world. The *Bluenose II* heeled over and swung around for our return run to Lunenburg.

Now experienced at traveling on a wooden sailing ship, I joined a group on a modern boat, the 45-foot *Cetacean Venture,* at Brier Island. We set out on the Bay of Fundy through light fog and choppy water on a quest for whales.

Carl Haycock, a wildlife researcher with BIOS (Brier Island Ocean Study), supports his work through these cruises. He briefed passengers about his research on humpback whales. "In summer many humpbacks come to feed in the Bay of Fundy after breeding in the Caribbean," he said. "Each has distinct markings, especially on its flukes. We send our sightings to compilers of the North Atlantic Humpback Whale Catalog at the College of the Atlantic in Bar Harbor, Maine. We have documented close to 200 individuals here, many with previous sighting histories in other areas of the western North Atlantic.

"We don't know the humpback's life span," Carl told me. "If we can identify calves, we can find out. Patch is the oldest in the catalog—about 16 years old. We also don't know how many calves a female might have. Istar, a grandmother, has had seven, and her third offspring is now calving. The whales don't sing here; they only do that in warmer waters, but there is vocal communication among them.

"We also record things like companionship. One year we saw a group of four females. The next year they all came back with calves. It's only a matter of time before we'll know about the humpbacks' social behavior.

"I can't promise that we will see whales," Carl told us, and we prowled the misty bay for more than an hour. Birds flew past or rode waves in flotillas. Carl pointed out black-legged kittiwakes, petrels, and sooty shearwaters that nest in the Falkland Islands. Suddenly a group of Atlantic white-sided dolphins leaped into the air in long arcs. Excitement rose, for these sociable and playful small whales are often companions to larger ones. Then dark, massive shapes slid past in the distance, barely breaking the surface.

"Humpbacks!" Carl shouted.

One of the gigantic mammals, perhaps curious about the boat, seemed fascinated by the excited human squeals its antics could elicit. First it cruised past a few times and lifted its tail. "Ooo," we cried. Several times it rose so near that spray from its blowhole spattered us. "Eeee," we squealed. The whale was hooked. For an hour it dived beneath the keel, drifted past with one flipper held high out of the water, sped by on its side with one enormous eye looking up at us, or slowly swam on its back, pale belly up. Three times it "spyhopped," rising out of the bay to meet us eye to eye. "Ahhh," we sang.

"I'm putting him on the payroll," Carl said. He noted that its dark, unfamiliar flukes marked the whale as one never sighted before in the bay.

The humpback's passes became slower, its appearances less dramatic. "I think he's saying good-bye," said Carl. For a long time we lost sight of our new friend and stood at the rail anxiously searching. Then a massive black tail rose slowly from the water, and the flukes unfurled to the sky. The whale began to dive deep into the ancient, drowned valley.

■ *French stronghold in the mid-1700s, Louisbourg guards an entrance to the Gulf of St. Lawrence. The fortress on Cape Breton Island prospered by supplying European markets with cargoes of cod. The town's stone ramparts knew war as well as commerce. Attacking from the sea, the British captured the outpost in 1758. Now restored as a national historic park, Louisbourg tells its story through local interpreters, called animators. One of them, Janet Sullivan-MacIntyre (opposite, in period costume of a serving maid), recalls the days when taverns here welcomed seafarers with clay pipes, playing cards, and casks of wine.*

FOLLOWING PAGES: Promontories rise a ■
thousand feet on Cape Breton. The isle's brooding heights bask in Gaelic traditions imported by Highland Scots in the late 1700s.

■ *Bright and lively capital of Nova Scotia, Halifax celebrates Canada Day.*
The national holiday, on July 1, salutes the 1867 union of provinces under
one government in the Dominion of Canada. The heart of Halifax is its harbor,
among the world's largest and the Maritimes' busiest. The British founded
Halifax as a port to rival French Louisbourg, and the capital still preserves their
spit-and-polish traditions. Among these are the 78th Highlanders (opposite) who
perform close-order drills for summer visitors. Along the downtown waterfront,
restoration has transformed early 19th-century warehouses—which once stored
the plunder of privateers—into gleaming shops, restaurants, and galleries.

■ *Nova Scotia's nautical ambassador,* Bluenose II, *plies Halifax Harbour. The vessel's*

predecessor won lasting glory in Canadian lore as a champion in international schooner races.

■ *Gabled buildings gaily painted reflect the European heritage of Lunenburg, in southern Nova Scotia. Landlubbers founded the waterfront town in 1753, but most gave up agrarian ways when they realized the sea offered a lucrative livelihood based on cod fishing off the Grand Banks. The town's craftsmen turned out many a tall ship, including the famed racing schooner* Bluenose. *Romantic images under clouds of sail, the wooden vessels carried on a brisk trade in salted cod with the West Indies. In his dory shop, Kim Smith (left) continues the Lunenburg tradition of handcrafting boats.*

FOLLOWING PAGES: Engines nod at rest on ■ *fishing craft at the village of Stonehurst—in a Nova Scotia scene reminiscent of a still life.*

■ *Verdant fields stretch to the brink of Cape Tryon (opposite) on Prince Edward Island, popularly called PEI. Cliffs breaking seaward reveal the fertile foundation of the province's farm economy, iron-rich soil oxidized to a rusty hue. Sixty lighthouses on the island serve notice that sea more than soil shapes PEI. Its early inhabitants, the Micmac, called it "land cradled on the waves." A jagged crescent in the Gulf of St. Lawrence between Nova Scotia and New Brunswick, PEI measures only 40 miles at its widest. Ferry crossings (above) to and from the mainland underscore the isle's dependence on maritime transport.*

■ *An arm of New London Bay links gentle pastures to the sea, seldom more than ten miles*

away on PEI. The island's rural charms inspired the beloved novel Anne of Green Gables.

■ *Fishing boats gather for the annual blessing of the fleet at Caraquet on the Acadian Coast, a peninsula in northern New Brunswick. When the British drove the Acadians out of Nova Scotia and southern New Brunswick in 1755, many settled here. Traditionally on the day before their fishing fleets set sail, towns along the peninsula hold a dockside festival. Women throw flowers on the water, and a priest offers thanks for the bounties of the sea. Opposite, captain John Vibert (in plaid shirt) and his crew haul in herring, prized for their roe. Often more than 300 boats crowd the same fishing area from sunset till dawn.*

FOLLOWING PAGES: The Rocks Provincial Park in ■ New Brunswick echoes the Maritimes' rugged beauty. Wind and wave sculptured the tree-topped flowerpots.

Scenic Shores of

■ *Cliff-top summer house at the end of the Gaspé Peninsula offers views of Percé Rock*

Quebec

By Jennifer C. Urquhart
Photographs by Michael Melford

(center) and the Gulf of St. Lawrence. Resorts and vacation dwellings line Gaspé's shores.

"Gulf that is still a sea, gulf that is already
a river as the salt water flows inland . . .
music of water and wind risen from the fathoms below
or following us from the high seas. . . ."

—Mia Matthes, Quebec writer, 1984

"*P*ARTONS, LA MER EST BELLE,*—Let us go, the sea is calm," the old song says. Eyes take on a faraway look. Faces soften. Arms of grandmothers draw small children near. Voices rise, filling the room with strains of an old and beloved air.

"*Embarquons-nous, pêcheurs*—Let us embark, fishermen . . . *Je vois briller l'étoile qui guide les matelots!*—I see shining the star that guides sailors!" And once again the cherished song recounts a tale of the sea and tragic death. It tells of a sudden storm. A father is drowned, a widow made. The song speaks of the perils that shadow those tied to the sea for their livelihood. It wells from deep in the heart of the French *patrimoine,* or heritage, that has endured on the Gaspé Peninsula of Quebec for some four and a half centuries.

I had joined a group of visitors in the parlor of an old farmhouse perched on a cliff at the eastern edge of the peninsula, now part of Forillon National Park. Jacques Cartier came ashore not far from here on his first voyage, in 1534, as he explored on behalf of the French king, Francis I. Like many early navigators, he was intent upon finding a westward route to the riches of Cathay. He never succeeded, but his arrival marked the beginnings of New France. And since then an abiding tie, at least in the minds of the Quebecois, has linked this region inextricably to things French.

Cartier's arrival is commemorated in the town of Gaspé by a monument and a large wooden cross similar to the one Cartier described in his journal: "We had a cross made thirty feet high . . . under the cross-bar of which we fixed a shield with three *fleurs de lys,* and above it a wooden board engraved . . . LONG LIVE THE KING OF FRANCE." Cartier is also honored in nearly every town and hamlet in Quebec, and he seems to lend his name to the primary thoroughfare of each municipality. Fleurs-de-lis adorn the blue-and-white provincial flag, not to mention the mud flaps on big provincial dump trucks.

The Gaspé Peninsula—Gespeg, or land's end, in the tongue of the Micmac Indians—may signify a beginning for New France, but it marks an end in

■ *Sunrise tinges the sea in tones of copper around Percé*
Rock. Forces of erosion alter its shape—as recently as
1845, two arches pierced the limestone formation.

89

SYLVAIN MAJEAU

the grand scheme of geology. Like the beak of a great bird, the tip of the Gaspé juts into the Gulf of St. Lawrence to form the eroded continental limit of the Appalachian Mountains.

*E*ARLY ONE MORNING I joined chief park naturalist Maxime St-Amour in his boat to round the tip of the peninsula. At first we cruised close to low, stratified cliffs that seemed to buckle, even slump into the sea. Cormorants perched on rocks near shore, hanging their wings out to dry. Farther along the coast, weathered limestone cliffs and talus slopes reached as high as 600 feet. It is a world in change; as we floated by, we could hear the peppering of the water and the narrow beaches as rocks dropped off the cliffs, precipitated by wind or water, or even birds. Sometimes whole sheets of the brittle sedimentary rock crumble, Maxime told me.

Kittiwakes, both adult and newly fledged, perched in tiny niches like delicate gray icons. Black guillemots, with scarlet mouths and matching red feet, were decidedly less saintly looking as they flipped bottoms up in the turquoise water. In the surf bobbed bright little harlequin ducks. "They always stay in the splash zone," said Maxime.

Approaching an isolated beach at the foot of the cliffs, we began to see seals, first the large grays, then the harbors. Perhaps two hundred seals stay here part of the year. This day most were in the water, popping their heads up to take a look at us.

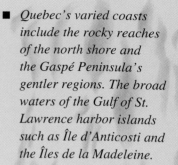

■ *Quebec's varied coasts include the rocky reaches of the north shore and the Gaspé Peninsula's gentler regions. The broad waters of the Gulf of St. Lawrence harbor islands such as Île d'Anticosti and the Îles de la Madeleine.*

Maxime promised that he could take us close to the colony. The shy harbor seals held back, but not the grays. "In French they are called *loups-marins*—sea wolves—because their cry is like a wolf's." Maxime made a howling sound. A responding howl drifted back over the water. We slowed and followed a steady course, apparently one not threatening to the seals. Maxime knocked sharply on the bottom of the boat. Suddenly the seals were following us. "They're very curious," he said. To me the profile of a gray seal is equine. As the animals rose and dived, snorting with nostrils flaring, I envisioned a herd of horses at full gallop—with Maxime as the wrangler. The seals looked disappointed as we left them to round Cap Gaspé, which rises high like the bow of a proud ocean liner.

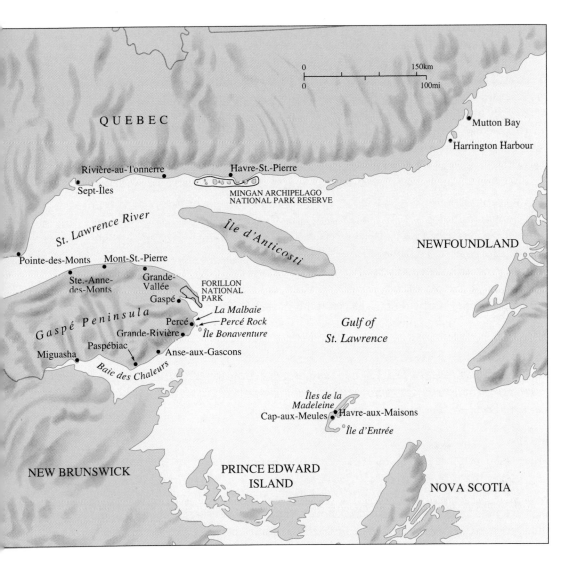

Quebec's southern maritime regions form a widespread, disparate area that includes the 170-mile-long Gaspé Peninsula, a thousand miles of north coast along the St. Lawrence River and the Gulf of St. Lawrence, and the remote archipelago of the Îles de la Madeleine, the Magdalen Islands, which traces a delicate arc across the center of the gulf.

Flowing for nearly 800 miles, the river drains the third largest watershed in North America. A marked transition occurs at its confluence with the Saguenay River. Here the depth of the St. Lawrence increases dramatically. Its waters meet and mix with the cold waters of the Labrador Current sweeping in from the sea, stirring up a nutrient-rich soup that supports life-forms ranging in size from the tiniest shrimps to the great blue whale, largest animal on earth.

The environment becomes both more estuarine and more marine as the waterway widens into the Gulf of St. Lawrence.

I had begun my wanderings in Gaspé on its southern shore, along the Baie des Chaleurs, the Bay of Heat. Cartier chose the name for the mildness of the weather during his visit in July 1534. Cartier was deceived—winters are hard here—but the climate along this shore is indeed gentler than on much of the northern coast. In a far corner of Chaleur Bay, in a watery cul-de-sac called Restigouche, British vessels defeated the last remnant of the French fleet in April 1760, ending France's political aspirations in Canada.

La Conquête. I would hear the term often in Quebec. There is only one Conquest here: the final defeat of the French by the British. A quiet little museum commemorates the event. In the dark space where I stood, hulking timbers re-create the interior hull of the French frigate *Machault,* blown up by the French themselves to prevent it from falling into enemy hands.

Nevertheless, many times in my travels on Gaspé and other parts of the Quebec coast I would encounter manifestations of the French grip. Sometimes the tug between French and English goes uneasily. Politics are announced in every front yard by the Quebec fleur-de-lis flag or by one bearing the Canadian red maple leaf. (At Percé I did run into a unique rapprochement: A boat flew both flags on one staff, back to back.) Along this south shore, though, English and French settlements mix. It's hard sometimes to know whether to say *bonjour* or good morning. But there is style here: What car owner wouldn't prefer a *salon de beauté d'auto* to a mundane car wash?

*I*N THIS REGION there is a decidedly Gallic interest in cuisine. I enjoyed local *fruits de mer*—shrimps, mussels, salmon, codfish. Cod surprised me—I never appreciated it until I ate it here, fresh, sweet, and moist. And *pot-en-pot,* seafood encased in the lightest of flaky pastry. I also enjoyed the traditional dessert of a rural society with large families and little money: a thick slice of fresh bread, slathered with candied maple syrup, topped with thick cream. And I once followed the advice of a young woman on a ferryboat and ordered *poutine.* "Quebec fast-food," she said. A mound of French fries, heaped with crumbled cheese, then drowned in brown gravy. Awful looking. Whoever concocted it must have been starving. Maybe I was, too—it wasn't bad. Colonel Sanders would not have been unhappy here either: His unmistakable red-and-white logo rides high in several towns at the Villa du Poulet, which serves *poulet frit à la Kentucky.*

Through the center of the Gaspé Peninsula runs the forest-cloaked spine of the Appalachians. I followed a winding road that climbed high through subalpine areas, then dropped down to the agricultural and resort areas of the Gaspé's north shore. Manicured gardens, capacious summer houses, and small cottages intermingle with pungent dairy farms along boulder-strewn beaches.

Villages and towns in this region bear names of a veritable galaxy of lesser-known saints: St.-Jean-Vianney; St.-Octave-de-l'Avenir; St.-Tharcisius; Ste.-Félicité; St.-Omer. The Roman Catholic Church has long been a powerful force here. Almost every little town seems dominated by an imposing church. "Flamboyant gothic" describes the architectural style of some spired edifices. Veiled in a lingering fog, the one in Ste.-Anne-des-Monts, on the north coast of the Gaspé, seemed merely ethereal.

I CHATTED IN THE TOWN with a priest, Father Roland Provost, a soft-spoken man in his mid-70s. At the time of the Conquest, there were only 65,000 French *habitants* in Quebec. Probably one reason that French culture prevailed is that the French were so prolific. "They would have very big families," Father Provost told me. "Sometimes eight, ten, fourteen, even twenty children. They needed them to help work."

Father Provost's European roots go deep, to the 1660s when the first Provost came from Normandy. His North American roots trace even farther back. "An ancestor way back then was an Indian woman, probably an Iroquois." Father Provost used to minister to the Micmac Indians along Chaleur Bay. One Sunday he announced to them, "I am an Indian. When I talk to you now, it's not only as a priest, it is as an elder." When he finished speaking, he said, "you could have heard a mosquito fly!"

In the early days the Gaspé was isolated. The road around the peninsula was completed only in the late 1920s. Cultures survived; the Micmac retained their language, and the English, Scots, and Acadians kept many of their customs. But one might as easily meet a man called Jones who speaks not a word of English as a man named Bouget who speaks no French. And how did some of the French-speaking habitants acquire their Scottish or Irish names? Father Provost surmises that a Scot might have been a British soldier who stayed after the Conquest—"I suppose he just got smart and found a nice French girl."

Farther along the Gaspé's north coast, flat land disappears. Forested mountains crowd the coast, then plunge into the sea. I found the water calm, though a chill wind gusted. Low tide exposed dark rock where black-backed gulls perched, feathers fluffed out and heads drawn in like old men with collars up against a gale. I followed a road at sea level, constructed at the foot of cliffs. One of the most vivid road signs I've ever seen warns drivers here of stormy seas with a silhouette of a tsunami-like wave curling above a skidding car.

At the village of Mont-St.-Pierre, precipitous cliffs coupled with strong wind patterns provide ideal conditions for a major hang-gliding center. Against the clear sky, a dense fog bank climbed rapidly from sea to cliff top, delineating perfectly the updraft that can keep a thrill-seeking flyer aloft for hours.

Such daredevil antics may seem crazy to some, but not to the gannets on the cliffs of Bonaventure Island. "Crazy" is what the French call these large seabirds—*fous de Bassan,* the crazies of Bass Rock. Big-boned, weighing about seven pounds, an adult gannet has a wingspan as wide as your outstretched arms. When aloft it is all aerodynamics, soaring or diving like a bullet for herring or mackerel. But with all that weight, it's not easy to get off the ground. That's where the updraft comes in. The birds run on their big black feet, as awkward as a diver's flippers, then attempt lift-off. Sometimes they thud to the ground in a heap before finally making it aloft.

One morning I headed out in a small boat with Lucie Lagueux to Bonaventure, off the end of the Gaspé. Lucie is chief naturalist for the park that encompasses the island and an eroding sedimentary formation called Percé Rock. Like much of this coast, Percé Rock is disappearing at a breathtaking rate, geologically speaking; it is considerably smaller than it was a century ago.

But the gannet colony is much larger. By 1887 the birds were decimated, clubbed by fishermen for bait. Now protected, some 50,000 nest here, making this the largest colony in the western Atlantic.

*J*OHN JAMES AUDUBON was clearly overwhelmed by a visit to a gannet colony on one of the Magdalen Islands. He noted in his journal in June 1833 that cliffs appeared "covered with snow to the depth of several feet. . . . They were birds we saw—a mass of birds of such a size as I never before cast my eyes on. . . ." This day, too, as we approached Bonaventure Island, the cliffs looked as if they were covered by a freak July snowstorm.

Depending upon the wind direction as you hike up the trail to the nesting cliffs, the introduction to the gannets on Bonaventure can be the smell of ammonia from guano, or the sight of creamy-white birds skimming over the spruce trees. Or it can be noise: The raucous squabbling of 50,000 birds is an impressive thing. Upon closer inspection, the white avian mass becomes a bewildering flurry of activity. Lucie explained some of the behavior—the bowing, the jabbing, the sky-pointing as the gannets nurtured their fluffy white young, fought, mated, or simply sounded off. Each family occupies about a square yard of fiercely defended territory. But even for birds the madding crowd's too much sometimes. One bird, arriving with a huge billful of grass, seemed truly perplexed and gazed around distractedly like a shopper at an enormous mall, wondering: "Now, just where did I leave that car?"

Birds brought Audubon to this part of the world, but fish have brought most people here. And fish have been in the region for more than 350 million years, according to findings along low cliffs on Chaleur Bay.

"This is our star, *Eusthenopteron foordi,*" said Marius Arsenault, pointing to a decidedly fishy imprint in a rock. Dr. Arsenault is paleontologist and curator at Miguasha, a small reserve encompassing the cliffs. The fossil he showed, and others unearthed from an ancient lagoon here, have helped reveal an important chapter in the story of the emergence of sea life onto land.

"In Miguasha we had two species of lungfish," Dr. Arsenault explained. "At first it was thought that these were the ancestors of amphibians, which were the first vertebrates to come onto land. But in the 1930s a Swedish paleontologist, Erik Jarvik, studied *Eusthenopteron* and came up with the idea that this type of lobe-finned fish rather than the lungfish was the ancestor of amphibians—and, therefore, of land vertebrates. This fish had the characteristics needed to come out onto land and evolve. It had internal nostrils. Its vertebral column was a little more robust because the animal had to lift its body. And if you look at the fin, you can see the leg. There are bones in there. It is the link between amphibians and fish. But, of course, we can't trace an ancestor absolutely, through 300 million-odd years."

*W*HETHER AMPHIBIANS descended from those species or not, fish are important here now, and salmon is probably the star. Indians depended on it; salmon fishing has lured princes and presidents to these waters for more than a century.

Cod commands a less exalted position, having sustained generations of ordinary folk in the Gaspé. I stopped at Paspébiac, the "Capital of the Kingdom of Cod." Many buildings of the Charles Robin Company are preserved as a historic site along the shore. Here, in the 1760s, Jersey islanders arrived, Charles Robin among them. Their trading companies gained control of the fishing industry and held fishermen and their families in what has been described as almost a kind of *esclavage*—slavery—of credit and debt to the company store, for boats and supplies. Today's problems are different, but no less complex. Many people in the region still depend on fishing for their livelihood.

At Gaspé, fisherman Leroy Leggo echoed the dire prognostications I had heard about the decline of cod. He blames the efficiency of big-time offshore fishing operations and sees his fellow inshore fishermen as "farmers of fish who take what we need. We were never efficient enough to take it all."

Exploiting species other than cod will not be easy. "You have to remember that the whole history here is based on cod," said Jean Boulva. "Cod has been the objective here, almost like oil is in other parts of the world."

I spoke with Dr. Boulva at the Maurice Lamontagne Institute, a modern research facility of the federal Department of Fisheries and Oceans at Sainte-Flavie on the north shore of the Gaspé. He explained the role of the institute, which he directs. "We specialize in marine sciences in what we all call the Inland Seas—including the Gulf of St. Lawrence," he told me. "You have very productive waters here. The gulf provides a quarter to a third of the total annual Atlantic fishery production in Canada—300,000 metric tons of a total of about 1,100,000 metric tons." The main aim is to have a lasting fishery, Dr.

Boulva said. Part of the problem is technology. "With improved fish-finder equipment, our ability to catch the fish has increased considerably."

Donald Leblanc would agree. I spoke with him at the Centre spécialisé des pêches in the town of Grande-Rivière. "The fishing is down," he said, "and there are too many licenses and boats and processing plants." Under the auspices of the provincial government, the center provides training in such traditional areas as fishing techniques, navigation, boat mechanics, and seafood processing. Why do you encourage young people to go into a declining industry? I asked. "It is a problem," Leblanc admitted. He sees hope, however, in the center's program and in aquaculture, the farming of the bounty of the sea.

*P*ROGRESS IN AQUACULTURE may be at hand. Salmon are being raised along the south shore. And for several years Aquatek Mariculture Inc. has been working to establish the production of mollusks in Chaleur Bay. Sylvie Bernier and Michel Moisan took me by boat to see their project.

"This year we will sell mussels," Sylvie said. "We plan to harvest 150,000 pounds and next year 300,000." The key to raising mussels lies in their life cycle. Reproducing mussels release eggs—as many as 12 million for some females—and sperm into the water willy-nilly. Fertilized at random, the larvae float until they attach themselves to a surface.

"They'll stick to anything that floats," said Michel. The trick is to supply that surface. In this case, long plastic strips are hung along lines to collect the mussels. Sylvie hauled a line out of the water. It looked like a rug of tiny mussels. "They stay on this for about five months, and then we put them into tubes called socks." The tube she showed me was covered with fingertip-size mussels. "After about two years these will be ready to harvest." The work on scallops is still experimental; new things don't have to start in a big way.

According to one Micmac legend, a grain of sand is enough. That is how the world began again after the great flood. When the land had been swamped, the Great Hare gathered all the animals around and asked who would go to the bottom of the sea for a grain of sand. Muskrat went down and came back with one, and from that was created a new land. In the Îles de la Madeleine—the Magdalens—such mythical origins seem entirely plausible. From the air, the islands look like fragile strands of sand flung across the sea. An early explorer called the archipelago *l'isle de Sable,* Island of Sand. Inviting beaches, in tints of pink and tan and edged with blue-green waters, stretch for miles. Bright red sandstone cliffs erode, constantly replenishing dunes and beaches.

Artisans and creators of sand castles use the stuff of these islands. But mostly the *Madelinots,* as islanders call themselves, and thousands of summer visitors simply soak up the sun on dunes or windsurf on waves warmed by Gulf Stream waters.

After sand, the first thing that impresses you in the Magdalens is the brightly colored houses. A rainbow of house paint scatters across the landscape: intense robin's-egg blue, periwinkle, apple green, forest green, persimmon, yellow, deep purple. The taste for vivid colors, some say, came with the Acadians, from whom most of the 15,000 islanders are descended.

That they are close-knit is revealed by the local telephone directory: Of its 46 pages, Leblancs fill nearly three, and Vigneaus and Arseneaus (with variant spellings) about two pages each; Cyrs, Boudreaus, and Lapierres each claim about a page and a half.

Two of the twelve main Magdalens remain fiercely Anglophone, and the most English of these is Île d'Entrée—also called Entry Island—the only one not accessible by road. One morning I took a boat over and wandered around. Steep hills rising high, treeless, and starkly beautiful were softened this day by summer's lush pasture and bright wildflowers. Most of the nearly 200 inhabitants subsist by fishing and raising cattle. A stubborn bunch the English five percent of the population must be—like the twisted, tenacious pines you see on some islands—to withstand all the French. Confusions do arise; it takes a while to realize that the towns of Cap-aux-Meules and Grindstone are one and the same, and that Havre-aux-Maisons is also House Harbour.

Now in his late 60s, Leonard Clark has deep roots in these islands and is an avid student of their history, particularly of local shipwrecks. He has already documented more than 700, but he thinks there were many more: "If there was no survivor, there would be no one to report the wreck. A lot of the ships in the early days tried to come over and back from Europe two times in a season." They had to come into the gulf early in spring when it was filled with ice. "In certain tide conditions the ice would open like big rivers," he said. "You could hardly see even on the clearest day. In fog or snow you might sail for miles without realizing the ice was anywhere near you. The ice would close with a change of tide, and you'd be trapped. Even cut in two."

The Magdalens presented an obstacle for ships. Leonard explained why. "If you had a heavy northeast gale, you wouldn't get much head. You're being pushed sideways. You might think you are 75 miles ahead, but in reality you have gone sideways and are only 30 miles ahead. When the ships turned, they'd put themselves alongside these islands.

"In late autumn of 1871 three ships sank on the same day. They were coming down the gulf, steering by dead reckoning, just by their compass and log. All of them thought they were on course." Leonard rolled out the map he has produced to document Magdalen shipwrecks and pointed. "The *Wasp* broke up here, and the *Halcyon* down here, and the *Peri* here."

Shipwrecks were horrifying. Hundreds died. Those lucky enough to make it to shore often succumbed to exposure or starvation. But some survivors did find help. Often they were obliged to spend the winter with their rescuers. Sometimes they stayed longer.

"The fact is that we got all sorts of groups landing here, and then you add a bunch of shipwrecked sailors," said Leonard. "They married the daughters. Got to know all the pretty girls in the community. So when a sail hove in sight in the spring, often many of these old tars and salts were dragging their feet. My great-grandfather was one of them. He was Finnish."

Since the 1950s a causeway has linked most of the islands. As I drove along it, late afternoon light silvered the water and softened grasses on dunes and hillocks to a golden green. Herons and ducks fed in the shallow marshes.

"A bunch of little birds, just looking for a place to set down and be left alone," Leonard Clark had described early settlers of the Magdalens. Real birds have set down in these islands too, among them the piping plover. Worldwide, piping plovers face extinction. Only 2,000 pairs exist; 35 pairs nest in the Magdalens. But increased tourism, off-road vehicles, and vacation cottages combine to threaten the dunes and beaches, critical for the survival of these tiny birds. Biologist François Shaffer and conservationist Patricia Bell are involved with a group dedicated to saving the plovers.

Audubon, while in the Magdalens, noted piping plovers as being "the swiftest of foot of any water-birds which I know, of their size." They *are* fast. Late one afternoon I met François and Patricia at a beach where they'd been observing a pair of nesting plovers. Even day-old chicks zipped along ahead of us.

Patricia showed me a tiny indentation in the sand containing a few bits of broken eggshell. That was it, home for the piping plover, totally vulnerable to vehicles, gulls, storms, footsteps. A storm hit the islands the next day, the end of a hurricane. I could not help but wonder, on my way back to the mainland, how those fragile creatures were faring against the lashing waves and winds.

Discovering on his second voyage that the St. Lawrence was a great river, Cartier reached a point high upstream where he encountered a friendly Indian village. Rapids barred further navigation. Cartier named the promontory there Mont-Royal, but that's about all he'd recognize of today's Montreal. Now a metropolis of more than two million, it lies at the juncture of the St. Lawrence Seaway, completed in 1959, and the navigable lower river. On the right bank, the last lock of the seaway from the Great Lakes feeds into the river. On the opposite side, the Port of Montreal stretches along 15 miles of riverfront.

"As far as we are concerned, we are part of the Atlantic seacoast," said Dominic J. Taddeo, president and chief executive officer of the Port of Montreal. Some 3,000 ships call at Montreal each year. In 1990, 22 million metric tons of goods moved through the port. "To the Montreal and Quebec economy, the port is worth over 1.2 billion dollars a year," said Taddeo.

In the old days, the port closed down in winter. "There were three things that meant spring for me," Taddeo reminisced about growing up in Montreal. "The budding of the trees, the opening of the baseball season, and the arrival of the first oceangoing vessel in port." That used to happen in late March or April. "Now we never close."

In those days there was terrific flooding in spring, when the ice packed up. Then the Coast Guard began breaking it up. "And," said Taddeo, "the spin-off of that was well, what do you know, the ships started coming through. The first one to penetrate was in 1962. Then lo and behold, in 1964 we are not closed at all!"

The task of keeping the river clear in winter for navigation below Montreal falls to the Canadian Coast Guard. Downstream at Quebec City, I boarded the icebreaker *Norman McLeod Rogers,* which was heading north for three months to supply outposts and install navigation aids in the Arctic. Such duties seemed worlds away on a hot July day. Ralph Hilchie and I leaned against a deck rail and watched people gathered in clutches on the pier — boyfriends and girlfriends, husbands and wives and children, solemn at facing several months apart. "It's pretty depressing leaving on a great day like this," said Ralph. "There's Agnes," he added, "our junior engineer. She's saying good-bye to her boyfriend. He's on another icebreaker."

*T*HE CREW released lines and the ship pulled slowly away. Other icebreakers at the pier blasted adieus on their horns. People waving on shore grew smaller. Later on the bridge, Ralph described his duties as ice services specialist for the cruise. There are 15 types of ice, he told me. Some types are called multiyear ice. When ice forms, it has little pockets of salt water. In multiyear ice, the salt eventually drops out, leaving freshwater ice, bright blue and incredibly hard.

Reports come in from reconnaissance airplanes about ice conditions in the north. Ralph charts the details for the navigation crew. In the past, planes would fly over and plot the ice on a chart, then fax it to the ships. Now he has a new device, the Star-vuc system. "Planes fly every two or three days, collect information with radar imaging, then transmit the information by computer."

The computer data are more complete. Black indicates water, white signifies land, and varying shades show different types of ice. "The object is to avoid ice. We could go through this," he said, pointing to a dark area, "but it would be slow, because there are traces of multiyear ice." On the printout I could see clearly where a ship had tracked through the ice. "If we hit it at high speed, we could damage the hull. Multiyear ice is the danger; it's frequently hidden among other ice types and difficult to detect. Icebergs we avoid entirely."

In winter along the St. Lawrence the problem is not multiyear ice; it is making sure that the ice keeps moving. This prevents flooding in the area from Montreal to Quebec City. "We do ice patrol first thing each morning to judge conditions," said Ralph. "The captain decides if any ice should be broken. In midwinter, at the Quebec City bridges, for example, ice funnels through this narrow channel in both directions with the tides, and it is important to ensure that it starts moving with each tide change. The last big ice jam was in January

1981. It had been minus 35° Celsius [-31°F] for a long time. The ice in the river jammed. It was so thick that the icebreaker could go no more than half a ship's length before getting stuck."

Hour after hour our sturdy vessel plowed through the water. In late afternoon, pink and gold streaked the sky. A few gray-blue clouds floated on the horizon. The next morning the ship's helicopter delivered me to the north coast of the St. Lawrence. Flying over, I could see the dark shadows of six whales swimming in close formation in the clear blue water, and the *Norman McLeod Rogers,* steady on her northward course, leaving me behind.

The region of the St. Lawrence called the North Coast begins at the river's confluence with the Saguenay, and in a highly civilized fashion—with a ruby-roofed grand hotel set in a jewel of a resort town, Tadoussac. In the harbor rides the graceful *Marie-Clarisse,* a semiretired 75-year-old *goélette,* or schooner. Once a freighter, she now takes passengers out whale watching. Several species of cetaceans, including the giant blue and an appealing little white whale called the beluga, frequent these nutrient-rich waters. Unfortunately, these waters are also rich in industrial pollution probably coming down from the Great Lakes. The belugas especially appear to have a high mortality rate, a result, it is thought, of that pollution.

"We call the belugas 'the happy imbeciles,'" says Robert Michaud, "because even though they're suffering from pollution, they're still playful." The animals are also called "canaries of the sea," for their wide range of vocalizations. Michaud notes these sounds as he studies the ecology of St. Lawrence whales with the Institut National d'Ecotoxicologie du St-Laurent. Part of the problem with the belugas near Tadoussac, Michaud believes, is that they stay longer in the river waters than other whales do.

Beyond Tadoussac, country-and-western music blasted earnestly on the car radio—as twangy in French as in English—"*Toujours dans mon coeur*—Always in my heart." Here the coast rapidly loses its patina of sophistication, becoming wilder, less groomed. Unadorned little towns and villages string along the coast, interspersed with strands of tree-edged, empty beach. In contrast to the fragile Magdalens, this part of Quebec's coast is rock-solid, firm as the bedrock Precambrian Canadian Shield that underlies it. Forests feed pulp mills. Immense dams and hydroelectric plants upstream hold back the largest of myriad rivers that cascade off the shield. Intricate webs of high-tension wires supply power to factories and urban centers. At Baie-Comeau a giant pulp mill dominates both town and waterfront. But all is not work at Baie-Comeau.

"A strong wind—it's *my* wind!" Raynald Claveau says. I join him, his son Luc, and five others to sail his 39-foot French-made sloop, the *Alexander Pickwick,* in offshore championship races held annually on the St. Lawrence.

As starting time draws near, shouts of "*bonne chance*—good luck" resound over the water. "*Cinq minutes!*—Five minutes!" Four minutes. Excitement grows. Three. We circle like wolves around the committee boat, jockeying for position, miraculously not colliding. A shot rings out. We're off! One boat forces us across her stern. We fall back. Up goes our genoa jib.

"*C'est beau!*" the skipper says as the sail unfurls and catches the wind. Now the wind dies. Are we sailing backward? Where is your wind now, Raynald? It's riffling the water far offshore. A scramble to get to it. Down with the limp genoa and up with the spinnaker.

"We got a bad start," says crewman Marc, with a Gallic shrug. "One day's bad, one day's good." Now we pick up a 22-knot wind. The boat cuts through the water with a crisp shirring sound. "*Préparez à virer!*—Get ready to come about!" says Captain Raynald. We turn smartly around a clanging bell buoy. "*Attention!*" Amazing teamwork—hauling sails, releasing lines, cranking winches—intense energy. I begin to understand the appeal of racing. Out comes the genoa again. "*Levez! Levez!*—Raise it!" We are heeled over almost to the waterline. Now we are in a dead heat with three other boats. Split seconds and little space separate us as we cross the finish. Who wins? It doesn't seem important. Attention turns to battening down the boat, looping lines, stowing winches and sails, all shipshape. With regret I leave my crew to other races and continue my journey along the coast.

I STOP AT SUNSET to see the lighthouse at Pointe-des-Monts blazing golden against the sea. Farther eastward, beyond Sept-Îles, the north coast again becomes wild and empty. At intervals, rushing rivers spill over the bedrock of the shield into the gulf. The spruce forest becomes scrubbier, twisted, seeming to grow out of the very rock. White lichens cover the rocks like snow. At the town of Rivière-au-Tonnerre, Thunder River, a stark church spire pierces the sky. The graveyard tops a high ridge at the edge of the sea.

Near Havre-St.-Pierre, Mingan Archipelago National Park Reserve encompasses 40 islands and numerous micro-ecosystems of animals and rare plants along a hundred miles of shore. The park is also known for formations of eroded limestone called flowerpots. I stroll on one island among these eerie guardians of the shore, layers of durable rock, left as softer rock eroded.

Patches of rain and sunshine turn the pavement before me into a disembodied silver ribbon as I head eastward. Then it really disappears. The end of the road. Beyond, along the north coast, Audubon's country truly begins, "so wild and grand . . . in its wonderful dreariness."

And here ends my journey along these shores. But the stark beauty of the place—the wildness, the surf-battered rocks, the clean-lined churches—will remain with me. And the cheerful warmth of the people that comes in a hundred ways—a gift of strawberries, the sharing of tea and cakes, a pot of steaming mussels around a kitchen table—these will stay, in the words of the country song, *toujours dans mon coeur.*

■ *Rounded butte and sheer cliffs flank the village of Pointe-Basse (opposite) on Havre-aux-Maisons, one of the Îles de la Madeleine, or Magdalen Islands. A large cross at the church on Île d'Entrée, also called Entry Island, commemorates five people drowned in 1988 while boating across the channel separating Entry from another island. Some winters bring easier contact; thick ice connects Entry—the only main island without a causeway—to the rest of the archipelago.*

■ *Rising moon glows above an apple green house in the Magdalen*
Islands. On the porch of a purple abode, a menagerie of pets basks
in the summer sun. Vivid hues brighten many houses on these
islands, perhaps to bring cheerful relief during long and severe
winters. This colorful tradition arrived with the Acadians, people
of French descent who settled here in the 1760s after their expulsion
from British-held Canadian territories. Acadians also brought
a rich musical heritage, which islanders have continued.

■ *Sweeping bay shelters Grande Vallée on the northern shore of the Gaspé Peninsula.*

River-carved valleys create coves for fishing villages. Forests support a timber industry.

■ *High-rise hatchery blankets cliffs on Bonaventure Island, near Percé Rock. Birds that nest here each spring—50,000 strong—form the largest gannet colony in the western Atlantic. Such close quarters require careful living: Breeding pairs fix on precise nesting sites retained from one year to the next. The birds use a dozen different movements to indicate intended activities and to alleviate conflict. By October, the colony disperses; the birds spend the following six months at sea.*

■ *Sinuous strata of limestone edge the
shore at Cap Bon Ami. Ever changing
from the seasonal freezing and thawing
that precipitates rockfalls, these cliffs
mark the easternmost reaches of the
Gaspé Peninsula. In summer, seals haul
up onto the beaches, now included in
Forillon National Park. Black-legged
kittiwakes and black guillemots perch on
tiny ledges and tuck into protected niches
in the cliffs to nest; multitudes of other
seabirds often swirl nearby.*

■ *Fisherman Armond Boulay relaxes after a day on the water. Laden with the day's catch—700 pounds of cod— his boat, the* Sylvain B. *(above), chugs back to dock in Gaspé Bay. Son of a fisherman, Boulay bemoans the decline of cod in the region. Fishermen, he says, must turn to less lucrative species like redfish (left). "It's 30 years I am fishing. We are paid about the same money for our fish as 20 years ago." Will his son, now seven, follow in his wake? "I hope not," says Boulay. "The fish are more scarce every year."*

■ *Blue-and-white provincial flag snaps smartly on the shores of La Malbaie. The white fleurs-de-lis, royal emblems of France, recall Jacques Cartier's arrival near this spot in 1534, and Quebec's settlement under the aegis of the French crown. Gallic pride runs deep, and French culture claims the hearts of Quebecois. Above, a fishing boat boldly displays its French name, which means "Dock of the Cove."*

114

■ *Grande dame of the north coast, the Hotel Tadoussac emerges from veils of fog and mist. A grounds keeper spruces up a lawn umbrella for the season. This spot, at the confluence of the Saguenay and St. Lawrence Rivers, has long served as a summer gathering place. Indians came from afar to barter copper, tobacco, walrus ivory, and other goods. Whites later established a trading post and one of Canada's earliest churches (foreground, above). Since the 1850s Tadoussac and other Gaspé and lower St. Lawrence resorts have enticed vacationers.*

■ *Beacon for mariners since 1830, the lighthouse at Pointe-des-Monts
guides sailors through the treacherous lower St. Lawrence. Replaced
by a nearby automated light, the old structure now houses a museum.
Downriver at Havre-St.-Pierre, the* Ferbec *docks to take on titanium
ore. For centuries the St. Lawrence has provided a major transport
route. Thousands of oceangoing vessels ply these waters each year.*

■ Twilight—and the end of the fishing season—bring tranquillity to Harrington Harbour. Samuel Cox (far left) tends his nets in this village of some 300 people on the lower St. Lawrence. At Mutton Bay, Harold Green (left) spreads split codfish on flakes to dry. Some 15 virtually roadless settlements dot this remote part of Quebec's coast.

FOLLOWING PAGES: A boardwalk affords dry passage ■ in a garden of flowerpots, eroded limestone formations, on Niapiskau Island in the Mingan Archipelago National Park Reserve. The lower St. Lawrence park shelters bogs and salt marshes with micro-communities of rare plants.

Icy Reaches of

■ *Scanning frozen waters for seal, an Inuit hunter forgoes harpoon for rifle.*

the North

By Thomas O'Neill

The modern weapon hints at the gradual eclipse of traditional ways in the Canadian Arctic.

"Hunting seals,
Hunting different seals,
Different ways of hunting different seals.
There is a joy in knowing the mystery of hunting seals."

—William Kalleo, Quebec writer, 1988

"*I* LOVE SEAL MEAT." Elijah Panipakoocho, an Inuit villager, spoke as if the words themselves tasted good. "Seal meat makes me warm inside," he said, "so warm that sometimes I can't sleep." Elijah had seal on the mind; he and I were standing on a shelf of sea ice five feet thick, looking down on a watery hole out of which minutes earlier a ringed seal had popped for a breath of Arctic air.

We couldn't move. A single footfall, even from far off, would scare the seal beneath the ice. Only the polar bear, with soundproofing fur between its footpads, can confidently sneak up to a seal's breathing hole. We could talk, though. Elijah must be hungry, I figured, as he proceeded to tell me how delicious caribou is, and eider duck, and arctic hare, and Greenland shark. He allowed that he didn't like raven or ptarmigan, and that big male seals could sometimes smell like gasoline. "I tell my sons," Elijah said paternally, "to eat fox and polar bear—it gives you good eyes."

In the Inuit worldview, animals are created for people to hunt and to eat. Elijah Panipakoocho is a hunter, and as such takes what the land gives. He lives on the remote northern end of Baffin Island in the native community of Pond Inlet, one of the northernmost settlements in the Canadian Arctic. From where we stood on the ice, at 72 degrees north latitude, the North Pole is 1,200 miles to the north, and the tree line is 1,000 miles to the south. Even in late June, with the flush of 24-hour daylight, we were bundled up against a piercing wind. Elijah, in his 40s, and short and powerfully built like most Inuit men, wore a homemade down parka with a hood ruff fashioned from wolf hair. Aviator sunglasses shaded his eyes from the blinding ice glare. As I listened to Elijah's roll call of edible animals, I remembered his telling me of ancestors who died of starvation on Devon Island, and of a great-grandmother who survived only by eating sealskin thongs. Hunger was not a lighthearted subject.

For 15 minutes we waited without success at the breathing hole, or *uglo* in Elijah's native language, Inuktitut. This was nothing. Elijah, who learned English on an oil-drilling rig, said that in the past he has stood for two hours in

■ *Airborne scramble of thick-billed murres unfolds with precision on Bylot Island. The hungry seabirds leave the skyscraper cliffs daily to feed miles from shore, where pack ice gives way to open ocean.*

BARBARA BRUNDEGE / EUGENE FISHER

bitter cold at an uglo. Polar bears may lie in wait for up to four hours. But Elijah was not hunting today. He was showing me his home territory on the frozen inlet between Bylot Island and Baffin Island—at 195,930 square miles the largest island in Canada. What had drawn me to this distant coast was the chance to see how the Inuit sustain their threatened culture by living, as their ancestors did, off the land and sea—and ice—and to observe the spectacular migrations of wildlife during the Arctic spring.

The notion that the Arctic climate, notorious for its severe windchill, prolonged dark winters, and freezing temperatures for much of the year, could support an abundance of wildlife seems at first glance rather hallucinatory. I scanned my surroundings at the seal hole and saw a desert. Everything looked formidably stark—the sea of ice, the bare granite mountains on shore, the awesome blankness of glaciers in the high valleys. Was that seal in fact a mirage?

As with every desert, however, there are oases, and few are more fabulous, more extravagant with life, than the Arctic floe edge, where landfast ice ends and open water begins. During the bright season between May and July, the receding ice becomes a platform from which one can watch along the nearby waters an unbelievable stream of migratory birds and marine mammals moving into the high latitudes to breed and feed. As I was eager to reach this ever-shifting viewing stand, Elijah gave up on the seal and went to rev up his snowmobile. I jumped aboard the long wooden sled he was pulling, and off we raced over the frozen sea.

Arctic Ocean

ALASKA — *Beaufort Sea* — *Banks Island*

U.S. CANADA

YUKON TERRITORY — *Victoria Island* — ARCTIC CIRCLE

■ *Much of the country's northern shoreline lies within the Arctic Circle. The vast Canadian Arctic Archipelago includes glacier-crested Baffin and Ellesmere, two of the world's largest islands.*

Before long we ran out of ice. The abrupt edge was flat and ragged like a torn piece of paper. It was unwise to stand too close to the rim lest a cake of ice break off and drop us in water so chilling we could survive in its grip only a few minutes. By craning my neck I could see the full measure of what we stood on—a chunky reef of greenish, pockmarked ice extending several feet below the waterline. Farther out, rafts of pack ice, having split apart in the warming weather, were floating like pieces of wreckage on the metallic gray waters of Baffin Bay. On the far horizon appeared pyramids, battleships, and skyscrapers, the forms of icebergs calved from tidewater glaciers in western Greenland, hundreds of miles away on the eastern side of Baffin Bay.

After traveling for six hours over an icy wasteland, I saw the gently

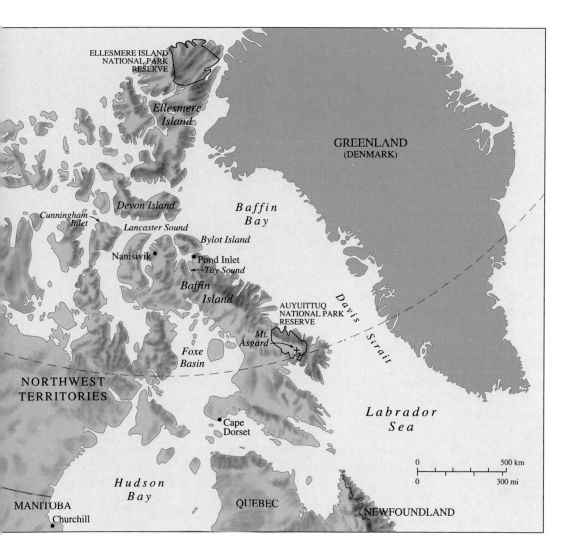

swelling sea at my feet as a pulsing organism, one that carried the ice on its back as a turtle does its shell. For hours I held vigil on the ice edge, watching animals appear from sky and water. Mobs of thick-billed murres—stocky, black-and-white seabirds—were constantly skidding to a landing on the water. Flocks of ducks, king eiders and common eiders, probably up from the East Coast of the United States, were flying low and fast, their heavy wingbeats sounding like the pounding of feet up a flight of steps. Arctic terns, white blurs in the air, dropped like stones into the sea to catch fish. They had flown a marathon from Antarctica. A frenzied splashing announced a group of harp seals that had surfaced and was now skimming across the water like a startled school of fish.

From the pack ice came a loud *poooff,* an explosive sound like that made by a steam locomotive. "Narwhal!" Elijah shouted. I spotted the fantastic beast, a mottled whale that looked silver and white in the sunlight. It was maybe 14 feet long and swam steadily toward the shore, its body looping in and out of the water like a sea serpent's. *Poooff, poooff, poooff.* Other narwhals were surfacing with loud, hoarse exhalations. It was the arrival of narwhals that had flushed the seals. Soon at least 20 of the small, gregarious whales were feeding not 50 yards away. When one of the big males dived deep under the ice, I could see the long, spiraled tusk projecting from his round head. Hard as it was to comprehend, this ivory tusk, which may grow to ten feet in length, and which is found on most adult males and on some adult females, is actually a living tooth protruding from the narwhal's upper lip. Its exact function is debatable. As natural history writer Barry Lopez has commented, "We know more about the rings of Saturn than we know about the narwhal." Scientists suggest that these mysterious marine mammals use their ivory tusks in displays of sexual one-upmanship and possibly as weapons.

I shivered with pleasure at the sights and sounds before me. Narwhals, the sea unicorns of fables, whistled, belched, and whinnied as they fed near the surface. About half of the world's 35,000 narwhals—found only in the Canadian Arctic and western Greenland—swim through Davis Strait into Baffin Bay in spring on their way to feeding and breeding grounds near Lancaster Sound. Sometimes the narwhals—and the murres—would disappear into the depths beneath the ice. What they dived into was a huge, agitated kettle of cod.

The arctic cod inhabits the center of a food web that forms when the sun returns to the far northern sky in February. The web begins on the bottom of the ice where shade-adapted algae grow. The algae feed shrimp-like crustaceans called amphipods, which feed the cod, which feed beluga whales that arrive in early spring. The system intensifies in June when the ice begins to break up and sunlight streams into the water. Pastures of phytoplankton—minuscule aquatic plants—bloom in the sea, turning clear water into a rich soup.

Tiny predatory animals called zooplankton now rise from the depths, the plant-eaters among them feasting on the phytoplankton, the carnivores devouring the newly fattened plant-eaters. The waters become even busier as the swarms of carnivorous zooplankton are attacked by arctic cod, which in turn attract hungry seals, seabirds, and narwhals. Elijah said that when you listen through a hydrophone lowered beneath the ice, the sounds of creatures, large and small, are as noisy as those in a rain forest must be.

Elijah and I were not the only interested parties out on the ice. All along the 20-mile length of this floe edge at the opening of Pond Inlet hunters waited. We had seen them: men huddled in tents smoking cigarettes and drinking tea; men leaning on sleds or fiberglass boats, their eyes fixed to binoculars; solitary figures pacing with rifles. They desired the narwhal. The spiral tusk fetches $125 or more a foot from Asian traders (the United States and many European countries prohibit the importation of raw ivory). More importantly, the narwhal provides *muktuk,* the layer of whale skin that is like candy to the

Inuit, who eat it raw. This cherished staple—it tastes like hazelnuts—is rich in vitamin C, a fact that enabled those explorers and whalers who adopted Inuit food to escape outbreaks of scurvy on their ships.

Only Inuit (about 27,000 live in Canada) are legally permitted to hunt narwhals, and then according to village quotas. Pond Inlet has a yearly limit of a hundred kills. The one animal the Inuit are forbidden to hunt is the bowhead whale, the only officially endangered animal in the Arctic. An estimated 11,000 once populated the Baffin Bay region; only about 500 remain, their numbers decimated in the 19th and early 20th centuries by American and British whalers.

Since Elijah and I were not shooting, the narwhals congregated in front of our safe neighborhood of ice. Gradually the hunters began to converge as well. I watched as a young man named Peterlosie approached the ice edge with a rifle, a grappling hook, and what appeared to be a suitcase. As the noisy narwhals continued to surface and dive amid the loose ice, Peterlosie reached into the case and took out a video camera. Elijah and I chuckled as the sentimental hunter shot home movies of narwhals. Switching from one pleasure to another, Peterlosie replaced the camera with his rifle, lining up a whale in his telescopic sight. It is not exactly target practice. The narwhals, when swimming in loose ice, expose themselves for only about a second and a half at a time. I wasn't keen to see the carnage and turned away. Loud concussive shots boomed from both sides. When I looked again, the surface was empty, and still bluish gray.

Later at our tent site, listening to a shortwave radio with its party-line chatter in Inuktitut, Elijah said that the hunters calling in sounded glum at not bringing in at least one narwhal. Sleep came grudgingly under the sunny midnight sky. I lay in my heavy bag for a long time listening to the echo of whale breaths and gunfire. The next morning the shortwave announced success, and we zoomed on the snowmobile to the nearest camp, where hunters were sharing fresh muktuk and seal meat.

*W*ITH HARDLY A WORD of greeting, Elijah began to eat with gusto. Some men were shooting cans lined up as targets on the ice. Others played cards. Wives and children were off exploring on foot, each group equipped with a stick used to gauge the thickness of the melting ice. An air of merriment flowed around the camp. My joy, I knew, sprang from the excitement of a wilderness experience. That wasn't the case with the Inuit, for whom only inaccessible mountaintops and glaciers are wilderness. Everything else, no matter how wild and daunting—the ice, the tundra, the cliffs, the mountainsides and valleys—is simply home ground, familiar and sustaining. The intense happiness of the floe-edge hunters and their families came from their sense of being at home.

Only in recent times has home suggested the existence of a permanent address. All Inuit 35 and older were most likely born at a seasonal hunting camp, in a *karmat,* a traditional shelter built of stone, sod, and whalebone. On our way to the floe edge, Elijah stopped and motioned toward a stretch of snow-covered shore. He was showing me where he had grown up in his family's winter camp. "The karmats are still there," he said proudly. "My brother and I take care of them. I know they must have been warm because I can still remember swinging in one with no clothes on."

These Inuit only began to live in towns rather than small settlements in the late 1950s. Some towns grew up around the Distant Early Warning radar sites installed by the U.S. and Canadian military. Most, however, sprang up in the wake of Canada's decision to centralize services—education, health care, welfare subsidies—for its aboriginal populations. Pond Inlet came into existence in 1959, when area families reluctantly disbanded their camps to live near the schools that children were now compelled to attend. Today, Pond Inlet is one of dozens of native—Inuit and Déné Indian—communities spread across the reaches of the Northwest Territories at the top of Canada. Little more than 50,000 people, half of them native, inhabit 1.3 million square miles, making the Northwest Territories one of the most sparsely populated areas in the world. So remote and weather-bound are the vast polar regions of the NWT that Arctic explorer Vilhjalmur Stefansson, traveling by dogsled, could discover large, previously unknown pieces of land as late as 1917. The coastline of the Canadian Arctic Archipelago wasn't precisely mapped until the 1940s, when, with the aid of military reconnaissance flights, a 500-square-mile island in Foxe Basin to the west of Baffin was noticed for the first time by non-Inuit people.

In these lands described by Canadian archaeologist Robert McGee as "the coldest, darkest, and most barren regions ever inhabited by man," native peoples have persevered for more than 4,000 years. Instead of defying the incredible environment, the Inuit have used it to their advantage, fashioning cold-weather clothing from caribou and polar bear skins, hunting sea mammals from the ice, building shelters—igloos—out of snow. Small, seminomadic family bands moved according to the seasons, catching fish and hunting caribou during the ice-free periods, taking seal and polar bear during the greater frozen part of the year. The people were poor only in the eyes of ignorant outsiders.

More than 30 years after its inception, Pond Inlet still seems temporary, like something left hurriedly on a doorstep. Much of the town of a thousand people sits on a bluff overlooking the waters of Pond Inlet. The inlet's name, like many of the place-names in the region, was conferred by British explorers—in this instance, by Sir John Ross and Lt. William Parry in 1818—who had come searching for the entrance to the Northwest Passage, the legendary trade route to China. Across the inlet looms Bylot Island, an austere, uninhabited mass of mountains and glaciers that buffers the town from the full fury of northerly storms. Utilitarian houses, most of them made of prefabricated materials, edge a few dirt roads under a welter of power lines. There is a runway for thrice-weekly jet flights to the "south," two general stores, an elementary and a secondary school, a mission church for the Anglicans and one for the Catholics, a handful of modest, overheated government buildings, and a simple hotel.

What's conspicuously missing is dogs. The heroic Eskimo dogs that pulled generations of Inuit families on sleds across trackless ice and snow, that could sniff out a seal's breathing hole in the dead of winter, that could corner a wounded polar bear, and that at the worst of times could feed a starving hunter, these hardy dogs have largely disappeared from Pond Inlet and most other Inuit villages. Snowmobiles have displaced them. From the days of their first extended contacts with Europeans in the 16th century, the resourceful Inuit have not been shy about exploiting the latest tools and technologies to increase their odds of survival. The *quallunat*—the "high brows," or white people—have brought nails, guns, knives, hatchets, saws, drills, telescopes, and now snowmobiles. Sheatie Tagak, a respected hunter and head of the local Hunters and Trappers Association, will speak fondly of dog teams, but he won't give up his snowmobile with its 503-horsepower engine.

"Yes, I miss the dogs," Sheatie told me in town as he prepared to go out to hunt a baby seal. (His wife would use its soft skin for making snow boots.) "Dogs don't break down, eh? But they go slower than the skidoos. They take a lot of time to take care of—to train and to get seal meat for, especially when you have a job." What gives Sheatie and other hunters pause is the rising expense of equipment. A hunter might pay as much as $10,000 to outfit himself with snowmobile, rifles, gasoline, and camping gear. To increase his options, Sheatie told me, he's begun to reassemble a dog team. A son works with the dogs after school. For the time being, however, Sheatie has adopted the unfamiliar and non-Inuit role of a wage earner who keeps specified hours at the local cooperative store where he works as an assistant manager. Strapped for time, Sheatie wants to make sure he can reach the floe edge in five hours, instead of the twelve it would take with dogs.

*D*URING MY VISIT in early summer, Pond Inlet looked like a ghost town. Practically everyone had taken off to collect bird eggs, hunt narwhal and seal, jig for fish, go camping with the family. No one wanted to waste the precious light-filled days. Temperatures were ascending into the exotic 50s. As soon as October the mercury would plummet to zero and lower (winter temperatures can nosedive to 40 below), and the sun would begin to set in midafternoon. In December and January the sun never scales the horizon. While most of the residents have come to enjoy the amenities of village life—modern heating, telephones, televisions, microwaves, washers and dryers—come summer, its charms become as dispensable as those of a hapless suitor spurned and abandoned for a truer love.

Among the few people still left in Pond Inlet one weekday was Caleb Sangoya, a government social worker. I was lucky to catch him in his office before he left to go "traveling," as the Inuit say. "Most of us employees in town use our vacations to go get country food," Caleb told me. "You people from down south call it a holiday. Most people here call it a harvest." According to Caleb and other leaders, hunting and gathering food from the land serve as anchors for Inuit culture, preventing it from being totally pulled into a whirlpool of selfish, materialistic values. Even so, Caleb saw worrisome symptoms. "There's less caretaking of the land, less attachment to it," he said soberly. "Everyone is getting too dependent on the government. In the old days no one took government assistance. We were living on our own. It's just like we once used all the parts of the animals we hunted. Now the skins and hides are often wasted; we use only the meat. In the old days brothers and sisters cared for the whole family and the community. Now I'm working only for my own things."

*T*HIS CULTURAL DISLOCATION and the loss of self-esteem that accompanies it are vividly evident to Father Guy Mary-Rousselière. Father Mary, as he is known to the townspeople, is a veteran missionary from a French oblate order, and a distinguished amateur archaeologist. For 45 years he has lived in close contact with the Baffin Island Inuit. I met the elderly priest in his rectory—a large trailer put up on blocks. "The people tell me," Father Mary said in his heavily flavored French accent, "that they feel as if they are sitting between two chairs and can't find their place. Many people are sad." Father Mary counts as a positive change the improved health care given the Inuit. But he bemoans the family-eroding influences of "drugs, booze, and television." Schools, in his opinion, offer the best lifeline to the culturally adrift. "Now the children are being taught Inuktitut again," he informed me, "where at first they were forbidden to speak it at school." The schools also offer courses in such traditional skills as building kayaks and sewing animal skins.

Twenty-five-year-old Kautak Kunnuk dropped out of school after eighth grade to hunt with his grandfather. For Kautak, as for most Inuit, the land is the key educator. It exists as a library-like repository of memories, skills, folktales, and customs. I had met Kautak through the Hunters and Trappers Association; he was the first Inuit who had agreed to guide me across the ice.

"If I hadn't worked with so many southerners on shrimp boats, drilling rigs, and at the lead and zinc mine [in Nanisivik, 50 miles west of Pond Inlet], I couldn't be open with a white man," he said to me early on when we had stopped in the lee of a frozen-in iceberg to make tea. What Kautak meant, I think, was that despite his people's reserve toward foreigners, he was willing to share his joy of traveling and to show me a few of the things he's learned.

Kautak drove a banged-up snowmobile while I rode behind with the gear in a long, box-like sled cobbled together out of wooden cargo crates. From a distance the landfast ice may look as smooth as a skating rink, but the real thing often is as rough as a logging road. Wind and tides pile up giant shards of ice along the shore. The surface takes on ripples and ruts. During the warm season, before total melt in late July, the icy plain looks like a shattered mirror, long, jagged fissures having pulled apart. The wider cracks slowed our travel. We often had to detour and wander the ice searching for a narrow place to cross. Or Kautak had to untie the sled, push it far enough across the lead so that the runners were bridging open water, and then, after jumping a crack with the nimble snowmobile, reconnect the sled and haul it across. I put my faith in Kautak (reading the ice is an Inuit specialty) and tried not to think that the mushy, melting ice was all that stood between us and water more than a thousand feet deep.

One day Kautak killed a seal. Rare was the time that we didn't see a ringed seal, the most abundant marine mammal in the Arctic, basking on the ice, and finally he picked up his rifle and shot one. His ancestors, Kautak said, believed that animals allowed themselves to be killed, and that to placate the spirit of a dead seal a hunter would offer a drink of water to the corpse. I asked if he followed that practice. "I don't believe in ghosts," he said with a flinch of embarrassment and dropped the subject. It was fascinating to watch Kautak dress the seal and to hear his commentary. First he carefully sliced away the skin, saying that he would offer the soft brown pelt to his mother-in-law to make waterproof boots. He tossed away the pale white blubber—"some old people still burn it to heat the house"—and the liver—"it has parasites in summer"—but kept the heart—"delicious"—which he sliced in half. Then he butchered the meat. The flesh has a purple-red color, a result of highly oxygenated red blood cells, an adaptation that allows seals to stay under the ice for lengthy periods. "I especially need a seal now," Kautak said as he carved, "because the broth we make from it will help my girlfriend lactate for our five-month-old son."

The subject of family obligations cropped up frequently. In an Inuit family, desires and needs are one, and any requests are expected to be honored. It is a radical notion of sharing. "My uncle asked for my almost-new skidoo and got it," Kautak told me. "My father asked for my sled and I gave it to him." I shook my head in amazement. "Can you ever say no?" I asked. Kautak smiled: "My mother asked for my firstborn, but my girlfriend refused."

Kautak did manage to keep one piece of the seal strictly for himself. After packing up the meat in a bag he fashioned out of the skin, he plucked out one of the seal's eyes, slit it open, and with deep pleasure sucked out the insides. He offered me the other one. I declined.

For all their savvy, the Inuit are not infallible on the ice. Things happen. Kautak and I were traveling one bright, windy day when we ground to a halt in front of a crack four feet wide. Kautak roared off on the snowmobile to look for a place to cross. Seeing him swing around and head back, I assumed that he saw the drop-off where ice had built up in front of a pool of meltwater. He hadn't. Kautak and machine sailed off the brow of ice straight into the pool. Before the machine could sink, Kautak, stunned but unhurt, scrambled ashore and with my help fished the smoking snowmobile out of the ice water. Of course it wouldn't start. After wringing out his socks and emptying his boots of water, Kautak shrugged off my concerns about his getting chilled and proceeded to dismantle the snowmobile's wiring, laying all the pieces on the ice to dry. He then contacted a nearby camp on the shortwave and requested some tools. A father and son soon appeared on a snowmobile. The teenager talked with Kautak. The father, a hunter I'd seen on the floe edge, crossed his arms, stared at the mess, and said little. It took three hours for the wires to dry and the snowmobile to start. Nothing to worry about, Kautak's efficient manner had suggested. Later, over the shortwave, Kautak joked with his girlfriend about the accident.

To court risk and excitement, many young men go egg collecting on the precipitous sea cliffs of Bylot Island. The one time I sensed trepidation in one of the Inuit came when a young hunter, after bragging about a recent polar bear kill, allowed that he was nervous about scaling the parapets, home to an enormous colony of seabirds. Sheatie Tagak had told me that some egg gatherers, before ascending, will swallow a raw seabird egg to give them courage.

At two o'clock one morning, the sun still shining brilliantly in one corner of the sky and the bleached rib of a new moon rising in another, Elijah Panipakoocho and I accompanied a crew of young daredevils to the bird cliffs on Bylot. To cross an extensive stretch of open water, we had to wedge a snowmobile, a sled, and nine passengers into a large freighter canoe. After a short zigzagging ride through shoals of broken ice, we regained solid ice near Cape Graham Moore. High, heavily faulted sandstone cliffs, chocolate brown in color, towered above us. Andrew Atagootak, 20, resplendent in a black jumpsuit with neon green and pink detailing and accompanied by his wife and one-year-old son tucked into the mother's parka, spent the boat journey and subsequent sled trip crowing to me about how he never wanted to sleep during the summer, and how town life seemed boring compared to all the adventures to be had out on the land. "Are you afraid, are you afraid?" he kept asking me eagerly.

All of us fell silent when the bird cliffs came into view. Even the brash young men were awed. For as far as the eye could see, seabirds, thousands and thousands of them, lined the ledges and crevices of the guano-stained mountain walls. Two kinds of birds were sharing the cliffs: thick-billed murres, sometimes called "penguins of the north" for their black and white feathers and the upright way they stand on land; and black-legged kittiwakes, small seagoing gulls. The noise stunned me. Shrill, excited cries, like the din of a playground, assailed our ears. When one Inuit clapped his hands, a storm of birds blew across the sky.

Four fearless men, packs on their backs, began scaling the escarpment, using ropes that had been secured at the top. About 500 feet up, the men let go of the ropes and began jumping from ledge to ledge like gymnasts, scattering birds and picking up large eggs. Andrew's wife and the girlfriend of another man stared up at them, visibly thrilled by the daring leaps and balancing acts. All the while birds shrieked and wheeled in a Hitchcockian frenzy.

While we watched the high-wire activities, Elijah told me an incredible survival story that had taken place long ago on these cliffs. Late one summer, a great hunter had been left stranded on the high walls by jealous enemies who had cut the climbing ropes. Made desperate by the approach of cold weather, he contrived a coat from the feathers of birds he killed with his bare hands. To sew, he turned wing bones into needles and muscles into thread. For food he collected bird eggs, and for drinking water he melted snow in the hollowed out corpses of murres and gulls. He lived on the rock wall until, five months later, he could climb to safety using handholds he made in the frozen ice and snow.

"Is that true?" I asked.

"Of course," Elijah answered. "The old people told us."

*B*ACK IN THE PRESENT, as the sun moved off the rock face and the air grew colder, the egg harvesters descended the cliffs. Their take totaled several hundred eggs, which they packed in crates with grass they had pulled from the mountainside. Everyone was tired but elated. A ritual of manhood had been observed. Later I would see some of the same youths in town, clowning around and making fools of themselves. They looked bored and idle, and younger than I had remembered. Being out on the land had made them grown-up.

Hunters and harvesters did not monopolize the ice. One day on the floe edge, when fog was blowing in as thick and obliterating as a dust storm, a dozen birders from the States and southern Canada made camp near where Kautak and I had stopped to wait out the weather. Few tourists undertake the long journey to Pond Inlet, but these amateur naturalists were on a mission to see and count as many bird species as they could in eight days. Each sighting would be relished since, as group leader John Coons, from Flagstaff, Arizona, told me, "in the tropics in a five-week trip you can find 500 species of birds; here in the vicinity of Pond Inlet during the same period, you will see 40 to 50."

To make up for the relative paucity of species, most of the birds that make an appearance do so in strength. Besides seabirds with their teeming cliff colonies, large populations of waterfowl, waders, and land birds descend upon the thawing tundra to begin their breeding seasons. I arrived on northern Baffin Island at about the same time that the greater snow geese were congregating. Most of the estimated 350,000 that migrate to Canada's eastern Arctic settle within a hundred-mile radius of Pond Inlet. I would watch them flying low over the tundra on Bylot Island, their honking calls startling in the deep silence of the place, their long white wings, tipped in black, shining in the bright sun like exquisite satin. They made a lovely pastoral scene, spread out on the sun-warmed vegetation, bending their heads to feed on insects. It is this springtime explosion of life—plant, insect, and oceanic—and the long, light-filled days for feeding that draw the feathered migrants to such latitudes.

Only a very few of the world's approximately 8,700 bird species over-winter in the Arctic; they include the common raven, snowy owl, gyrfalcon, rock ptarmigan, hoary redpoll, Ross' gull, and ivory gull. They all have a heroic aura. At the time I met the birders near the floe edge, they had only hours earlier witnessed a rare bowhead whale feeding so close to the ice edge that they could have petted the huge marine mammal. But even as I was voicing envy at their fantastic sighting, the birders seemed much more elated at having just seen on the pack ice a flock of all-white ivory gulls.

*T*HE ARCTIC ANIMAL I craved seeing was the polar bear, the great white hunter that prowls the sea ice for ringed seals, invades the tundra to gorge on berries, and plunges into the sea to chase fish. In the high Arctic, the population of the *nanuq*—valued by the Inuit for its thick pelt and savory flesh—has generally remained in a healthy state since hunting quotas were imposed in 1967, soon after the introduction of snowmobiles. The nanuqs eluded me, however. Probably the number of people camping on the floe edge for the narwhal hunt had persuaded the evasive, well-camouflaged bears to keep to the floating ice pack, where they have been known to yank live narwhals out of the water.

Just because I never sighted a polar bear doesn't mean that I failed to sense the creature's formidable presence. Every night on the ice my Inuit guides took a rifle or a shotgun to bed in case a hungry bear should show up. Fresh tracks were usually reported on the shortwave. Kautak explained in grave detail how I should play dead if ambushed by this predator. Elijah in particular loved telling tales about the power and the guile of the polar bear. He told me how he had once seen a bear carrying a small walrus in its mouth, and how another time he had witnessed a bear making a large ball out of ice, which it used to brain a sleeping walrus. "Polar bear hunts all the time, rarely sleeps, always looking for seal," Elijah told me, his admiration explicit for this way of life.

The kinship that Elijah feels toward the polar bear, and to a lesser degree toward the arctic wolf and the snowy owl, stems from the fact that all of them survive by hunting. For Elijah it is an honor, as well as a practical matter, to hunt polar bear. Hunting is not a blood sport to the Inuit; each kill is an affirmation of a passionate covenant between humans and the environment. "I remember the first animals I killed," Elijah once said to me, "the first rabbit, ptarmigan, seal. It's like the first time with a girl—you never forget."

Once when we were watching for narwhals at the ice edge, a thick pelt of fog hanging above the ice, I asked Elijah about the qualities of a good hunter. "A good hunter," he answered after a long silence, "takes care of his family. If someone in the community is hungry, he has enough meat to give him. A good hunter knows how to survive. So many things have changed, but the weather never changes. The winter is always cold and dark. The white man comes in spring and says all is fine. He never comes in winter, when we have to survive. If the plane couldn't bring in gas and food, the good hunter would survive."

Winter was far from everyone's mind in late June. The ice was turning softer; cracks were widening; pools of water were spreading. The ice surface had the blue-and-white complexion of polished marble. The warmth of the season and the annual breakup of the ice made for a slow, bruising ride as Elijah took me away from the floe edge and up Tay Sound on Baffin Island. In a month all the ice, seemingly so permanent, would be melted, and the long, chill, nine-month season of the snowmobile would give way entirely to the brief, warm, three-month season of the boat.

In the meantime, the frozen highway between Bylot and Baffin bore its steady traffic as families on sleds and snowmobiles streamed toward outlying camps. At the end of Tay Sound, Elijah and I found seven large canvas tents set up on the gravel shore. Beside one tent caribou meat and bright orange fillets of arctic char were drying on lines. Most of the campers had gone out on the ice, where they had arranged themselves along both sides of a freshly opened crack and were jigging for char. Everyone, from slow-moving elders to frisky youngsters, was pulling up large fish right and left from the dark water, taking advantage of the season's migration of char from inland lakes to the sea. Gulls and jaegers and loons noisily crisscrossed the sky above, eager for discards.

That this spot had long been productive became apparent on the walk Elijah and I took on the tundra behind the shore. We saw lichen-encrusted tent rings, old whale bones, and small rock enclosures that had been built as fish caches. Rectangular fish traps, made of stones, were visible in a crystal-clear stream. Whether these remains are a thousand years old or a hundred is hard to tell. I bent and drank from the delicious stream. I couldn't remember the last time I had safely done that. "There must have been a lot of meat here," Elijah exclaimed. "No sugar, no coffee, no flour, just water and meat."

Before we returned to town, Elijah drove me on the snowmobile over tundra and into the mountains to another oasis, a seven-mile-long body of water called Iqaluit, or Fish Lake. Clattering over rocks and splashing through puddles, we took a route that paralleled a river course along which stood rocks piled up to resemble human shapes. These were *inukshuks,* scarecrow-like figures that had been used by hunters to direct the flow of migrating caribou herds. Once on the frozen surface of the lake, Elijah pointed to a rumpled caribou skin. "Wolf kill," he shouted over the roar of the engine.

Then Elijah and I turned predator. Standing on the rim of the ice, near the head of the lake, we dipped our hooks into a pool of recently opened water that was so clear we could see the char as plainly as if they were swimming in an aquarium. The char were massing for migration, and we could pick out the ones we wished to bite our hooks. At one point Elijah and I, swept away by the abundance of fish, turned to each other and laughed, the short, wild sounds echoing off the bare rocks on shore. Here we were, at the top of the food web.

■ *Fronting the shore of Baffin Bay, the Inuit settlement of Pond Inlet perches at the northern end of Baffin Island, a larger-than-Sweden hump of tundra, fjords, and bleak mountains. Here within the Arctic Circle, the summer sun sets reluctantly, and the cutting wind seldom loses its icy edge. Most of the year Baffin Bay lies under thick pack ice. Warming thaws bring respite—only in August (above) can residents expect the arrival of supply boats.*

BARBARA BRUNDEGE / EUGENE FISHER

The Inuit, once scattered in hunting
camps, now reside in villages, but
still survive mostly on their skill as
hunters of caribou, narwhal, char,
and their mainstay, netsik—ringed
seal. They zealously pass down
hunting skills and other traditions
of rugged independence to their
children in the hope of preserving
their culture. Under August's
midnight sun, hunter Daniel
Qitsualuk (above) shows his two-
year-old son the ageless source
of Inuit sustenance, the sea.

■ *Pack ice cracking apart forces hunter
Daniel Qitsualuk to leap for safety.
He made it, but Joe Koonoo (left)
didn't. His snowmobile sank when he
tried to skid it across a meltwater gap
to shore. Fellow hunters rescued him
and his machine. In winter Baffin
Bay's thick ice becomes the Inuit's
hunting grounds. In June the pack ice
begins to melt and break up. Sudden
fissures can trap unwary hunters on
large rafts of ice that float out to sea.*

■ *Formidable peaks of Mount Asgard beckon a
hiker on the downhill sweep of Turner Glacier.
The 6,600-foot mountain on Baffin Island ranks
as the highest in Auyuittuq National Park
Reserve. Throughout the area stand* inukshuks,
*like the one above, their stones arranged to
resemble humans with arms flung wide. These
cairns mark trails, caches of food, and
hunting and fishing sites, or help spook caribou,
driving the animals into a hunters' ambush.*

■ *PRECEDING PAGES: Usually whiplashed by wind, blossoms of willow
herb nod on a calm day, a rarity in Auyuittuq's Weasel River Valley.*

■ *Soapstone art depicts Inuit ways and Arctic wildlife. Hunters probably sculptured images such as this six-inch polar bear as talismans to appease the animals' spirits. A six-inch mask of a woman, carved in traditional style, makes a fashion statement. Until early in this century, many Inuit women stitched their skin with sooty sinews, tattooing linear patterns to enhance their beauty.*

■ *Cold pink marble comes to life for two young admirers of native sculpture. This drum dancer stands as the largest stone carving produced by Inuit artists. Craftsmanship runs strong in their culture. On Baffin Island, the town of Cape Dorset successfully bases its economy on the production of fine art. The stone-cut creation "Night Crossing" (right) came from the hands of local lithographer Mary Pudlat. Cape Dorset carver Pee Mikigak (above) works on a stone block of stylized owls.*

FOLLOWING PAGES: August thaw shatters pack ice off Canada's ■ northernmost land, Ellesmere Island. Greenland lies only 25 miles away.

■ *Mother's howling perks up the
ears of a tundra wolf pup.
Peaked ears, short muzzles, and
shaggy coats reduce the loss of
body heat and help the animals
withstand Arctic temperatures.
Wolf packs roam Ellesmere
Island in search of migrating
caribou, their main prey in spring
and summer. The wolves also
hunt arctic hares. Bounding
across the tundra on Ellesmere,
a hare (above) stands erect for
several kangaroo-like hops to
spot possible predators. The
hare's white coat provides
camouflage during snowy winter
months, but seems to call out like
a dinner bell in early summer.
Soon it will turn brown to
blend in with the surrounding
terrain until snowfall.*

FOLLOWING PAGES: Luminous in morning light, a glacier-calved ■
iceberg drifts seaward past austere mountains on Baffin Island.

■ *High-flying flukes reveal belugas swimming in Cunningham Inlet off Somerset Island. In summer the whales molt by rubbing against sand and gravel in river shallows. The scrubbing also gives their skin an extra luster of whiteness. July warmth coaxes a bearded seal (opposite) to sunbathe on an ice floe.*

FOLLOWING PAGES: The polar bear stalks the Arctic as ■
one of the world's most aggressive land carnivores.

FRED BRUEMMER (BOTH)

The Majestic West

■ *Craggy headlands spill down to the sea at Long Beach in Pacific Rim National Park.*

Coast

By Cynthia Russ Ramsay
Photographs by James A. Sugar

Mountains, fjords, and misty forests bring beauty to Canada's rugged western edge.

" . . . the sunlight filters so greenly into shadow . . .
nothing is focused sharply among these ghostly islands
where even the present seems sometimes like a memory. . . ."

—Viola Wood, British Columbia writer, 1978

O N A FINE SUMMER DAY, when the conifer forests cast green shadows on the blue waters and distant snowy peaks glistened against a cloudless sky, I set out to explore Canada's island-fringed west coast. It was the salmon season, and the fish, fresh from their feeding grounds in the open ocean, were jumping, their silvery forms flashing like mirrors in the sunlight. To prey on the salmon, killer whales had arrived in large numbers. At times the vapor spouting from their blowholes caught the light, and rainbows shimmered in the small plumes of mist, touching the sea with magic.

Perhaps the best time was evening, for in July the sun lingers at land's edge. On the long, lonely beaches, pale driftwood logs glowed with the luster of gold. The lengthening rays burnished the sea lions basking in their rookeries and the shaggy grizzlies prowling the estuaries for salmon. The sun flared on moss-covered branches of Sitka spruce, silhouetting the giant trees with light.

In the city of Vancouver, the sunshine had brought crowds to beaches and waterfront promenades, whose panoramas sweep from mountains to the sea. In the harbor, heavy traffic churned furrows of foam in the sparkling water, as ferries, freighters, fishing vessels, cruise ships, floatplanes, sailboats, and barges pursued the commerce and pleasures of coastal life in British Columbia, Canada's Pacific province.

Such radiant days seem even more so after a long spell of mist, rain, and pea-soup fog, when the landscape is reduced to a gray monochrome dominated by the darkness of the sea. Canada's wettest days are in British Columbia, where on October 6, 1967, a record 19.26 inches of rain fell near the village of Ucluelet in one 24-hour period. Yet in this landscape dominated by rain forests, there are arid places within the rain shadows of the high mountains where cactus grows. Victoria, the provincial capital, averages a mere 28 inches of rainfall a year. The city boasts of roses blooming in December and golf the year round. Its climate, the mildest in the country, lures retirees from all over Canada.

■ *Set between the Coast Mountains and the sea, the city*
of Vancouver boasts a life-style of year-round
recreation—boating in summer and skiing in winter.

Hilary Stewart, a writer-artist known for her books on Northwest Coast Indian cultures, wouldn't wish for any other climate. "The rain nourishes our magnificent forests. It makes the lovely ferns and mosses. It fills the rivers, enabling the salmon to go upstream to spawn," she says.

In the old days, the big winds and big waves of winter ushered in a sacred season for the Indians. Families and guests would sit around the fires of ceremonial houses, where masked dancers in the flickering light brought the supernatural world to life.

"We really had a nice time. The big house would be filled with the sounds of chanting, and we feasted on dried salmon and food gathered in summer and fall," says Kwakiutl matriarch Agnes Cranmer.

CANADA'S PACIFIC RIM stretches from the Washington State border and the Strait of Juan de Fuca north to Alaska. As the eagle flies, the distance is about 500 miles. But 5,500 islands and islets, countless coves, jagged peninsulas, and deep fjords extend the shoreline to some 16,000 miles. It is a steep, mountainous coast, wrinkled and rumpled by pressure from three of earth's tectonic plates, which converge here. Glaciers that blanketed the land until 12,000 years ago bequeathed to it the rugged beauty of rock chiseled by ice.

The maze of waterways, with twisting straits and inlets, has made the B. C. coast a paradise for sailors, kayakers, and other boaters. The coastal seas sustain one of the world's great commercial fisheries, teeming with halibut, cod, herring, and five species of Pacific salmon—coho, king, sockeye, pink, and chum. To these bountiful waters tens of thousands of people come each year to fish, casting for the "smileys," the big ones anglers dream about.

There are also nightmarish hazards that have earned the outer coast the epithet "graveyard of the Pacific." Since Spanish explorer Juan Pérez anchored his frigate off Vancouver Island in 1774 and British explorer James Cook sailed into Nootka Sound four years later, hundreds of ships have foundered in the perilous waters. Ocean swells brewed by storms as far away as Japan rampage across the open ocean and mix with waves generated by local gales. Sometimes boats roll so much that it's easier to walk up their doors than through them.

The sea is tamer in the Inside Passage, the north-south marine highway that lies between the mainland and the islands of the coast and extends from Washington State to Alaska. But the narrow channels, sometimes less than 2,000 feet wide, take skillful maneuvering.

"Coming from ocean shipping to this is like negotiating city traffic after driving in the desert," said William McKechnie, in his thick Scottish burr. Captain of the *Queen of the North,* the ferry that makes the 315-mile passage between Port Hardy, on Vancouver Island, and Prince Rupert, on the mainland, he invited me to the bridge during the 15-hour run north.

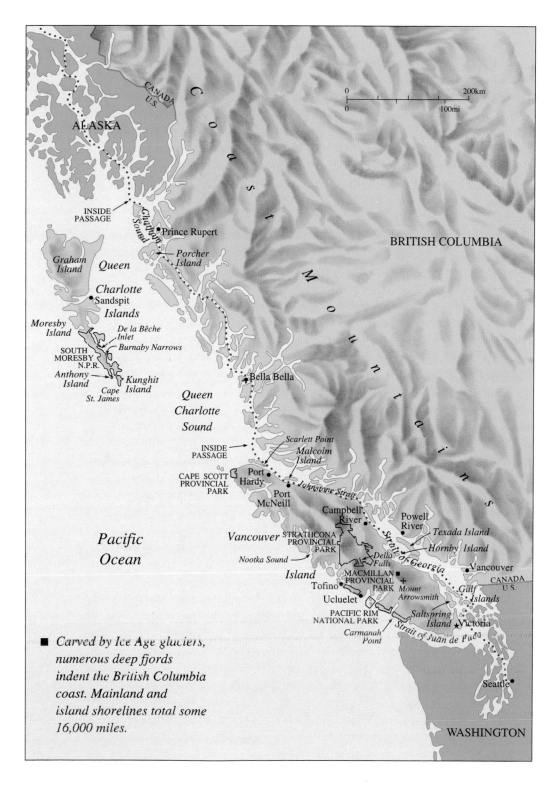

ALASKA

CANADA U.S.

Coast

BRITISH COLUMBIA

INSIDE PASSAGE

Chatham Sound

• Prince Rupert

Porcher Island

Graham Island

Queen

Charlotte

• Sandspit

Islands

Moresby Island

De la Bêche Inlet

Burnaby Narrows

SOUTH MORESBY N.P.R.

Anthony Island

Kunghit Island

Cape St. James

Bella Bella

Queen Charlotte Sound

M o u n t a i n s

INSIDE PASSAGE

Scarlett Point

Malcolm Island

CAPE SCOTT PROVINCIAL PARK

Port Hardy

Port McNeill

Johnstone Strait

Campbell River

Powell River

Texada Island

Hornby Island

Vancouver

STRATHCONA PROVINCIAL PARK

Nootka Sound

Della Falls

Strait of Georgia

Vancouver

CANADA U.S.

Island

MACMILLAN PROVINCIAL PARK

Mount Arrowsmith

Gulf Islands

Tofino

Ucluelet

PACIFIC RIM NATIONAL PARK

Saltspring Island

• Victoria

Carmanah Point

Strait of Juan de Fuca

Pacific Ocean

Seattle

WASHINGTON

0 ——— 200km
0 ——— 100mi

■ *Carved by Ice Age glaciers, numerous deep fjords indent the British Columbia coast. Mainland and island shorelines total some 16,000 miles.*

"Fog never stopped the old steamship traffic in the Inside Passage, though it may have slowed it down," he said, recalling the days when freighters plied this route, bringing mail, groceries, and passenger service to logging and fishing outposts. "The masters of those boats in the early 1900s navigated through thick weather by tooting the ship's whistle through the narrow channels. Those old-timers would sit by the open window and judge the distance from shore by the echo," he told me, scanning the waterway with binoculars.

For most of the way, the ferry traveled through a corridor of trees. Hemlock, spruce, and cedar crowded the slopes. Gray spires striated the density of green, where ancient cedars were slowly dying from the top down. Flashing against the foliage were the white heads of bald eagles. Porpoises rode the bow wave for a while before disappearing into the depths. This exceptional span of steep forest and deep water is also home to humpback whales, wolves, and the legendary white "ghost" bear of Tsimshian Indian folklore, an extremely rare subspecies of black bear called the Kermodei.

In one of the ferry's dining rooms I met George Housty, a Heiltsuk chief. George was returning home to Bella Bella after a visit to Vancouver. "It takes me four days to get tired of the concrete city. I like window-shopping, but I feel pushed by the crowds," George said. "In the city everything is partitioned. Where I come from there are no fences."

Mostly George talked about the Indians' struggle to retain their tribal identity despite pressures to assimilate.

"I was only nine when the Department of Indian Affairs sent me off to a residential school. There we were punished for talking in our own language. I would get a strapping for not speaking English," he said. "When my wife and I speak Heiltsuk, my children and grandchildren don't understand us. How can we know who we are and where we belong without knowing the language that carries our legends and history? But now we've started teaching it in the schools, and these days the young people don't feel embarrassed to learn old dances and songs."

George's grandfather had been a part-time hand logger. "He used a boat to skid logs into the water, so he could only work real close to shore," George explained. "It was something to do between fishing seasons."

We were about 40 miles south of Alaska's Panhandle when the ferry eased past a log boom two blocks long and docked in Prince Rupert. Japanese freighters were loading wheat and corn at the new high-tech, computer-run grain elevators, which have put Prince Rupert on world shipping maps. The city of nearly 17,000 is also the port for commercial fishermen of the north coast, who sell their catch to the five canneries lined up along the waterfront.

For me the docks were a gangplank to the small, remote communities that lie beyond the reach of roads, where people fence their vegetable gardens to keep deer out and are never too busy to stop and talk. Aboard the *Sun Chaser,* a 40-foot ketch, I set out across the harbor with skipper Dan Wakeman, who quickly proved his competence by catching a 14-pound coho salmon; it fed us sumptuously for the four days of our trip.

Our first destination took us away from the vista of the mainland's Coast Mountains and south across Chatham Sound to mountainous Porcher Island. By the 1920s settlers had cleared land and built cabins along the north end of the island. These pioneers logged in winter, fished in summer, raised some vegetables. Today nearly all the homesteads have been abandoned.

*H*AROLD CAMPBELL bought his property, a small peninsula on Porcher Island, from descendants of an original settler. We found Harold, a fisherman for most of his life, aboard his gill-netter, tied to his dock at Welcome Harbour. "Fishing is not a bad way to make a living," he told us. "March and April is the herring season, and June through September I'm chasing salmon. Then it's time to overhaul the engine and mend the nets. A new engine costs about $6,000. But buying toys for the boat—that's where the big money goes," he said, pointing to the electronic sounder and the radar scanner. "A boat's never finished till it's sunk."

Harold, his wife, and their two sons are the only residents of the small peninsula with its snug harbor on one side, a black gravel beach on the other, and a lush rain forest in between. It was lovely strolling in that forest in the green shade of giant trees, with an eagle chirping occasionally in the canopy high above. Red salmonberries, ripened to a delicate sweetness, grew in big clusters that brightened the shadows. The tang of salt and the fragrance of moist earth, pungent with decay, filled the air. A narrow trail, maintained by Harold, made it easy to walk on the forest floor, which was choked with ferns and thickets of salal and snarled with fallen timber. Downed trees were "nurse logs" that bristled with saplings and other new growth. In this way, a tree that may have lived a thousand years would serve the forest for another few hundred.

On the beach, the waves rolled ashore lazily, their slow rhythm enveloping the solitude. The lack of company doesn't bother Harold, who was raised with his brother in a lighthouse.

"I was 17 when I got a driver's license, but I ran my own fishing boat when I was 13. When other kids were working on cars, I was working on outboards. I've never been on a baseball or basketball team, and to this day I'm not interested in sports. I've never been tied to doing what the crowd does. I could always be my own person."

Leaving Welcome Harbour, we chugged around the island to Oona River on the east coast of Porcher, bucking a two-knot tidal current. It was typical fjord cruising with fickle winds, so Dan relied on power rather than sail.

"It's not bad steering," he said, "but you always have to be on the lookout for driftwood logs, especially the 'deadheads'—ones that have absorbed water and are partially submerged."

Rafts of driftwood come to rest on B. C. beaches, looking like leftovers from a giant's game of pick-up-sticks. Wedged into rock crevices far above the high tide line, the logs reveal the power and height of the waves that hammered them there. Much of this debris—billions of board feet of wood once worth billions of dollars—has strayed from log booms and logging operations. Says the manager of one company, "We can lose as much as 20 percent of what we cut."

Like everyone else who docks at Oona River, we had to wait for high tide. But the 30 or so free spirits who populate this community don't mind. What matters to them is not having to punch a time card. By the time we could bring our skiff to the dock, the community's daily coffee break was in full swing around the big table in Fred Letts's kitchen.

Fred has fished for crabs, worked in the sawmill, built boats, logged, and done whatever else came up ever since he drifted in with the tide in 1923. Now crab fishermen are hauling in one crab per pot instead of 20, and hand loggers can't simply pick off a few trees.

"These days you need a permit to log," said Fred. "When you locate a claim, the government puts it up for bid and gives the permit to the highest bidder. Guys who just scratched out a living have been put out of business.

"But Oona River is a good home base for people who don't like rules and regulations. Any damn fool can live in the city. But here everyone has to know how to cut firewood, tie a knot, run a boat, operate a VHF radio—even the kids. Out here youngsters have to pull their own weight—they're partners," said Fred, talking above the chatter of the VHF marine telephone in the kitchen. A goodly number of people in the "bush" and on boats keep these radios on most of the time. "It's more than a telephone; it's used for distress calls, and by listening in, you might save someone's life," explained Fred.

One channel runs weather reports continuously. Others carry private conversations. The staccato broadcasts are the Muzak of the coast, letting everyone know who's going to town and who's having a birthday. But when a troller tells his buddy where fish are biting, he'll use their private code.

Though the community still remains a far cry from cosmopolitan Vancouver, Oona River's pioneer life-style is rapidly fading. Residents recently built a helicopter pad so that a medical emergency can be quickly evacuated by chopper to a hospital on the mainland, and hydroelectric power will soon replace household generators.

At the remote southern end of the Queen Charlotte Islands, an archipelago some 60 miles west of Prince Rupert, there's not much that reminds you of the 20th century. There are no power lines, no chain saws, no gas stations or other facilities in the verdant wilderness of 138 islands called South Moresby. Unique life-forms—rare flowering plants, the smallest saw-whet owls, the largest black bears in Canada, and species of birds, shrews, and mosses found nowhere else—make this misty, storm-lashed fragment of the country's western shores a naturalist's dream.

Access to the South Moresby region is not easy. A few fishing vessels anchor in deep coves; a few private boats and charter yachts make South Moresby their special destination. Otherwise, it is off the beaten track. Once the southern Haida Indians launched their dugouts from here, raiding and trading along the mainland coast for hundreds of miles. Their villages had also been ports of call for 19th-century British and Yankee traders who made fortunes in sea otter pelts, but the animals were virtually exterminated, and the last of the southern Haida villages was abandoned by 1889.

From the Sandspit airport in the Queen Charlottes I flew south by floatplane to De la Bêche Inlet, where I boarded the *Darwin Sound II,* a 71-foot ketch. Her skipper, Al Whitney, is a former professor of environmental studies. He and his wife, Irene, conduct excursions to this coastal strip of islands and islets. "Nature, art, and anthropology expeditions under sail," Al calls them.

Over dinner with Al, archaeologist Steve Acheson, cook Simon Fawkes, and five others, I learned about the 15-year struggle to have South Moresby set aside as a national park. It was one of the most publicized confrontations between conservation and commercial interests in British Columbia. The turning point came in 1987, when lumbermen rushed to log 1,200-year-old trees in the area. Public outcry and media fanfare forced the federal and provincial governments to place a moratorium on the logging. In 1988 South Moresby was set aside as a proposed national park reserve while an agreement is worked out with the Haida, who claim all the Charlottes as their homeland.

Al reminded us that some of the trees were old when Shakespeare was penning his plays. "Logging is our primary industry in British Columbia," he said. "Some say it brings in 50 cents of every dollar. But it's the pace, scale, and waste of indiscriminate logging that we have been fighting. Would anyone think of tearing down the Tower of London as a make-work project?"

*N*EXT MORNING we arrived at Burnaby Narrows, a shallow channel where low tide reveals the marvels of intertidal life. Wearing gum boots, we discovered a mosaic as vibrant as a stained-glass window—but this masterpiece was a quarter of a mile long. Sea urchins like purple pincushions, orange sea cucumbers, pink coralline algae, red rock crabs, scallops with purple mantles studded with orange eyes, and bat sea stars a vivid blue, red, or fuchsia spread the ocean floor with life. Sea lettuce, an acid green, lay wetly on a shiny black pebble shore, where clams squirted water like miniature geysers.

Two days later we sailed down the west coast of Kunghit Island with a 21-knot wind filling the mainsail and genoa jib. We were headed for Cape St. James on the island's southern tip, one of the windiest, wildest points on Canada's west coast. In spring and summer it teems with seabirds—part of a population of a half million migrants that converges on South Moresby to breed.

The influx into Saltspring Island arrived with an agenda—pursuing a hobby or craft, or enjoying retirement in a halcyon place.

Some 80 miles to the northwest is Hornby Island, in the Strait of Georgia, and many who went there in the 1960s and '70s just drifted in and hung out. For shelter they built imaginative driftwood structures using lumber found along the beach. One circular house on pilings was built with only $500 in materials and "four years of scrounging."

By the '80s the houses had been upgraded and enlarged, and what may .have started out as little more than a barn with baling wire repairs now has sliding glass doors and skylights. Attitudes have also changed, and former hippies are now involved in a spectrum of careers.

"SOME OF US here on Hornby still nurse a little nostalgia for the blend of idealism and hedonism that was part of the hippie life-style," declared Richard Martin, a resident curmudgeon with a curly black beard. Once a professor of philosophy in Washington, D.C., he now wires houses for a living and has become an authority on local botany.

Richard deplores what has happened to Hornby's volunteer fire department. "In the old days everyone would rush to the scene with a shovel and a bucket. Then some guys felt the need to make their mark, so they professionalized the fire brigade. That sort of thing drives the frontier spirit out."

I had met Richard at the Vorizo Café, a popular meeting place for locals, who are a breed apart from the summer people from Vancouver. While tourists looked for bargains in the small craft shops and stalls around the plaza, Richard and his friends discussed island affairs. Everybody seemed to have strong opinions, but when a golf course was proposed recently, it was an issue that mobilized the community into an uncommon consensus to vote it down.

"Usually, between the iconoclasts and the anarchists, it's hard to get us to agree," said Richard.

The bluffs at Hornby's Helliwell Park are a perfect vantage point for watching the sunset. A thick purple haze had enveloped the forested expanse of nearby Texada Island and the billowing contours of the mainland. To the west, on Vancouver Island, a pearly pink cloud trailed across Mount Arrowsmith, where Richard often hikes from sea level to high meadow—from algae to alpine flowers, as he puts it—to be alone with his thoughts and his plants. Before long the shimmering sea dissolved into an inky blackness without boundaries except for white ripples of foam on the rocks below and the twinkling lights of the towns strung along Vancouver Island's eastern shore.

I returned to Vancouver Island to continue my journey. Beyond the town of Campbell River, clusters of motels, restaurants, and shops disappeared, and for almost a hundred miles the road wound through an evergreen empire where logging is king. My island-hopping by ferry resumed at Port McNeill, and I headed for the trim village of Sointula on Malcolm Island, a 25-minute run into Queen Charlotte Strait and well north of the Gulf Islands.

Sointula, which means "place of harmony" in Finnish, began with turn-of-the-century dreams of a utopian society in which no one would own anything individually and everyone would work for the common good. The language of those visionaries is still spoken in Sointula. The blood of those Finns who were escaping Russian tsarist oppression or the miserable conditions in B. C. mines flows through the veins of the fishermen who now steer out of Sointula's docks. The experiment in socialism failed, but Sointula has grown and prospered as a workingman's town. People will take over a parking lot to hang their gill nets to repair them; they will block traffic to land a boom of logs and move it across the road. No one objects because work is what matters in Sointula.

*T*ED TANNER REMEMBERS fishing in the 1930s, when salmon were plentiful and prices were low—35 cents for a whole sockeye weighing 6 pounds. "Now they get 2 dollars a pound," Ted told me.

He used to enjoy fishing because there was no boss telling him what to do, but he doesn't miss it now. "There are so many rules and regulations it would be a nuisance. I just miss being younger."

I asked Ted what makes a good fisherman. Without hesitation he replied, "Someone who doesn't need much sleep. If you can think like a fish it helps—like knowing how a fish travels with the tide. Sometimes it just takes a pair of binoculars and watching the other guy. Maybe it's easier now with all the electronic gear, and maybe in the old days the fish found us."

Down the road at the Rough Bay Ritz, the talk at the tables was also about fishing. The banter was lively, but no one bragged. David Renwall, age 21, said he felt as if he'd been fishing forever. Someone reported that Dave had just brought in a hundred fish. His reply was rapid: "Three hundred would have been better."

I learned more about the fisherman's trade and the importance of such things as carrying a fresh handkerchief or starting the day off at a particular spot. Superstitions of this sort restrict one Sointula mariner to two beers a day—when fishing. And all the Ritz crowd agreed that if a fisherman is just going through the motions without concentrating, he won't catch fish: "Your feelings go down the line."

No residents of Canada's western shores are more fascinating than the 190 or so salmon-eating killer whales that cruise Johnstone Strait, a narrow passage between Vancouver Island and the mainland, northwest of the Strait of Georgia. These powerful five-ton predators live in close-knit family groups. The males are mama's boys, remaining even as adults with their mothers, which may live 80 years. The family, which also includes the female offspring, hunts, plays, and rests together for life.

"It's a weird social system without precedent among mammals," said researcher John Ford, curator of marine mammals at the Vancouver Aquarium. John and I were aboard the *Lukwa,* one of the charter boats that provide whale-watching tours.

"The animals are very sociable and chatty, keeping in touch with each other through a dozen or so distinctive sounds that range from metallic screams to raucous squawks. We know they communicate even when they are out of sight of one another, over a distance of at least four miles," John said as skipper Jim Borrowman steered his vessel closer to Vancouver Island's rocky shore, where the whales go to chase down salmon. "They flush the fish out of the kelp beds," Jim explained.

*E*XCITEMENT ROSE among the passengers as Jim spotted the mist of a whale's blow. He lowered a hydrophone into the water, and through a speaker in the boat we heard a series of clicks that sounded like static. "They use that for echolocation to zero in on their food," said Jim.

Someone spotted the black triangle of a dorsal fin knifing through the water, and then another and another. In silence we marveled at these sleek black-and-white behemoths rolling effortlessly through the sea, rising to the surface and diving in one continuous undulating movement. Two passengers had come from Europe for this moment. They were not disappointed.

I spent the final days of my journey at Tofino, a fishing village on the western shore of Vancouver Island. Much of this outer coast is accessible only by sea, just as when British navigator George Vancouver charted the region, covering 65,000 miles from 1792 to 1794. I walked the nearby beaches rimmed by forests, listening to the pulse of the ocean against the sandy shore. In the calm of a golden sunset, I paddled out into the harbor in a sea kayak. Bobbing like a cork in the light swells, I sat for a while thinking about all that I had seen in a month of travel. I remembered the words of Mark Hobson, an artist in Tofino.

"People live on the coast because they passionately love its unique blend of forests, mountains, and sea. If we lost our jobs, we would do almost anything to stay here. For most of us, it is not the work we do that is the priority. Instead, it's being able to live in a place surrounded by incredible beauty."

I understood what he meant.

Afternoon tea remains a tradition in Victoria, the genteel ■
provincial capital, nicknamed "a bit of England." Some
shops specialize in British goods such as china and tweeds.

■ *Quiet moments around a fire
end the day for campers at Upper
Campbell Lake in Strathcona
Provincial Park. This Vancouver
Island sanctuary protects cougar,
black bear, and elk, and
encompasses glaciers, alpine
peaks, and Canada's highest
waterfall—1,443-foot Della Falls.
Below, fresh salmon and garden
vegetables provide the ingredients
for a gourmet cookout on a beach
strewn with driftwood logs near
the town of Powell River on the
mainland's Sunshine Coast.*

FOLLOWING PAGES: Woodland trail knifes through ferns and shrubs crowding ■ a rain forest floor in Cape Scott Provincial Park on northern Vancouver Island.

■ *Protected from the logger's chain saw, centuries-old Douglas fir trees survive in MacMillan Provincial Park on Vancouver Island. Fir, giant cedar, Sitka spruce, and hemlock attract the timber industry, which has stripped much of the 280-mile-long island's primeval forest. After clear-cutting (below), stumps and slash litter an area near Cape Scott Park. Logging steep slopes may cause landslides, soil erosion, and silted streams, adversely affecting fish and other wildlife.*

■ *"Coastal travellers pass down inlets devoid of human habitation," writes author Howard White, "until it seems like they are moving down a long, green corridor of time itself, dropping backward into some primeval age when the earth was devoid of sentient life." Such vistas unfold before passengers on the ferry* Queen of the North, *as she churns down the Inside Passage between Prince Rupert and Port Hardy. A fleet of 38 ferries connects 42 ports of call in British Columbia. A Cessna (opposite) commands a bird's-eye view of the village of Tofino and the tide-washed solitudes on the west coast of Vancouver Island.*

183

■ *Floatplanes based in Prince Rupert link far-flung villages and logging camps on the north*

coast with the coal and grain port. Many communities remain inaccessible by road or car ferry.

■ *Far from highways and city conveniences, a congenial group gathers for muffins and cribbage in Jean Martin's kitchen at Hunts Inlet, a small Porcher Island community. Homegrown onions dry in a woodshed at Oona River on the island's east coast. A kitchen counter holds a sole destined for artwork rather than supper. Coated with dye, the fish will be used as a stamp to decorate fabric.*

■ *PRECEDING PAGES: Sleek killer whales, weighing about five tons, summer in Johnstone Strait and prey on its bounty of salmon.*

■ *To keep the beacon bright in fog or storm, Al Tansky cleans the windows of the Scarlett Point Lighthouse on the Inside Passage. The light at Carmanah Point (opposite) marks the entrance to the Strait of Juan de Fuca. A network of 50 lighthouses—36 of them manned—helps mariners negotiate the perilous coast.*

■ *Dramatic wooden masks reflect the artistic traditions and the rich cultural heritage of the Haida, native people of the Queen Charlotte Islands. Goat hair forms the eyebrows on an eagle spirit mask fashioned from cedar and painted red. An abalone-shell lip ornament, or labret, adorns the sculptured face of a woman. The striking image of Ga-giit, a legendary Haida wild man, has Chinese coins for eyes, cows' tails for hair, and plastic spines around vivid blue lips.*

MASKS BY ROBERT DAVIDSON (ABOVE AND OPPOSITE) AND GLEN RABENA (BELOW);
PHOTOGRAPHED BY FRANS LANTING / MINDEN PICTURES

■ *Sunset flares on a beach in Cape Scott Park. Bountiful tidal waters draw more than 400,000*

anglers to the coast each year; other visitors come for the dramatic scenery and tranquil setting.

Notes on Contributors

JAMES P. BLAIR joined the Society's staff in 1962. During the past three decades, his photographs have been featured in more than 40 NATIONAL GEOGRAPHIC articles. Jim's concern for the environment found scope in the Society's book on federal lands, *Our Threatened Inheritance*. He previously covered the Maritimes for the Special Publication *Exploring Canada from Sea to Sea*.

JOHN EASTCOTT and YVA MOMATIUK have journeyed to many environments in their careers. They wrote and photographed an article on the Inuit for NATIONAL GEOGRAPHIC in 1977. Two years later they collaborated on a chapter about Louisiana's Atchafalaya Swamp for the Special Publication *Exploring America's Backcountry*.

MICHAEL MELFORD, a free-lance photographer, lives on a farm in New York. For the Special Publication *The Emerald Realm*, he traveled to the Costa Rican rain forest, an area he had visited earlier on assignment for *Life*. His photographs have appeared on the covers of *Newsweek, Life,* and *Connoisseur.*

TOM MELHAM has logged more than 20 years on the Society's staff. His writing assignments have taken him from Alaska to Antarctica. Author of *John Muir's Wild America*, Tom has written chapters for *The Emerald Realm*, *The World's Wild Shores*, *America's Seashore Wonderlands*, and many other Special Publications.

THOMAS O'NEILL, a member of the Society's staff since 1976, is the author of *Back Roads America: A Portfolio of Her People* and *Lakes, Peaks, and Prairies: Discovering the United States-Canadian Border*. He has contributed to many other Special Publications, most recently the chapter on the American tropics in *Hidden Worlds of Wildlife*.

CYNTHIA RUSS RAMSAY, a staff member since 1966, enjoys exploring the outdoors and took special pleasure in British Columbia's mix of mountains and sea. She has written chapters for more than a score of Society books. Those with environmental themes include *Nature's World of Wonders, America's Seashore Wonderlands*, *The Emerald Realm*, and *Alaska's Magnificent Parklands*.

GENE S. STUART's assignments in North America as a staff writer have taken her from Alaska to Honduras. She is author of *America's Ancient Cities* and *The Mighty Aztecs*. With her husband, staff archaeologist George E. Stuart, she wrote *The Mysterious Maya*.

JAMES A. SUGAR is associated with the Black Star photo agency. He has free-lanced as a writer and photographer for NATIONAL GEOGRAPHIC since 1969. His book assignments have included *America's Sunset Coast* and *Railroads: The Great American Adventure*.

JENNIFER C. URQUHART, a staff member since 1971, has gone on many writing assignments for Special Publications, including ones that took her to Canada's western provinces of Alberta and British Columbia. This book gave her a first look at eastern Canada and the opportunity to meet the lively Quebecois.

Acknowledgments

The Book Division is especially grateful for the assistance of Andre C. Aubin and Frank LaFlêche of the Embassy of Canada; the provincial and territorial tourism offices; and the federal and provincial Departments of Energy, Mines, and Resources; Environment; Fisheries and Oceans; Forestry; and Transport.

We also wish to thank the individuals and organizations named or quoted in this Special Publication, and those cited here: Carl Amos, Atlantic Geoscience Centre, Don Barr, Elisabeth B. Booz, Lorraine Brandson, Brier Island Whale and Seabird Cruises, Ltd., Peter D. Brown, Ken Campbell, R. Wayne Campbell, Ernie Christmas, Bas Cobanli, Robert W. Dalrymple, Paul DeMone, Alain Dufour, Carole Duguay, Amy Evans, Brent Fredrick, Jean-Louis Frenette, David Frobel, Bruce Garrity, Nick Gauthier, Dennis Godin, Lynda Hanscome, David Harley, Nancy Harris, Peter J. Haughn, Al J. Hobbs, Ken Hoffman, Wendy Jakobsen, David Johns, A.J.B. Johnston, David Knickle, Serge Labonté, Antonio Landry, Frédéric Landry, Francine Lane, Jan Lemon, Bernard Major, Malibu Club, Wayne McCrory, Aynsley McFarlane, David Morrow, Maria Muehlen, Helen Jean Newman, Norm Pascoe, Wayne Patton, Lynne M. Perry, Potlatch Arts, Claude Richard, Terry Ryan, Janet Skinner, J.W. Stephens, Steve Suddes, Jon D. Taylor, R.B. Taylor, Debbie Thorne, Dorothy E. Thorne, René Trépanier, Jack Troake, Paul von Baich, Stan Wedge, Fran Williams, Tony Williamson.

Composition for this book by the Typographic section of National Geographic Production Services, Pre-Press Division. Set in Times Roman. Printed and bound by R. R. Donnelley & Sons, Willard, Ohio. Color separations by Graphic Art Service, Inc., Nashville, Tenn.; Lanman Progressive Co., Washington, D.C.; Lincoln Graphics, Inc., Cherry Hill, N.J.; NEC, Inc., Nashville, Tenn.; and Phototype Color Graphics, Pennsauken, N.J. Dust jacket printed by Federated Lithographers-Printers, Inc., Providence, R.I.

Index

Boldface indicates illustrations.

Additional Reading

The reader may wish to consult the *National Geographic Index* for related books and articles. The following books may be of special interest: Alaska Geographic, *British Columbia's Coast: The Canadian Inside Passage*; Andrew Hill Clark, *Acadia: The Geography of Early Nova Scotia to 1760*; Tim Fitzharris and John Livingston, *Canada: A Natural History*; John and Janet Foster, *Adventures in Wild Canada*; Pierre Fournier, *Quebec Establishment: The Ruling Class and the State*; Hubert Guindon, *Quebec Society: Tradition, Modernity, and Nationhood*; Sam Hall, *The Fourth World*; Farley Mowat, *The New Founde Land*; Patrick O'Flaherty, *The Rock Observed*; Frederick Pratson, *Guide to Eastern Canada*; Bryan Sage, *The Arctic and Its Wildlife*; Miyuki Tanobe, *Quebec, I Love You: Je t'Aime*; Sarah Bird Wright, *Islands of the Northeastern United States and Eastern Canada*.

Library of Congress CIP Data
Canada's incredible coasts / prepared by the Book Division. National Geographic Society. Washington, D.C.
   p. cm.
   Includes index.
   ISBN 0-87044-829-3
   1. Coasts—Canada. 2. Canada—Description and travel—1981–
I. National Geographic Society (U.S.). Book Division.
F1017.C37 1991
917'.00946—dc20   91-19420
                          CIP